MORE THAN
A GAME

Michael Moynihan is an editor with *The Irish Examiner*. He has written many books and co-produced documentaries such as *The Game, Christy Ring: Man and Ball* and *GAA Nua*. A regular contributor to TV and radio, he lives in Cork with his wife and children and is a member of Glen Rovers St Nicks.

MICHAEL MOYNIHAN

MORE THAN A GAME

THE GAA AND WHERE IT'S GOING

Gill Books

Gill Books
Hume Avenue
Park West
Dublin 12
www.gillbooks.ie

Gill Books is an imprint of M.H. Gill and Co.

© Michael Moynihan 2025

978 18045 8203 9

Designed by Typo•glyphix
Edited by Jane Rogers
Proofread by Heidi Houlihan
Printed and bound in the UK using 100% renewable electricity at CPI Group (UK) Ltd
This book is typeset in Adobe Garamond Pro.

The paper used in this book comes from the wood pulp of sustainably managed forests.

To the best of our knowledge, this book complies in full with the requirements of the General Product Safety Regulation (GPSR). For further information and help with any safety queries, please contact us at productsafety@gill.ie.

A CIP catalogue record for this book is available from the British Library.

5 4 3 2 1

For Marjorie, Clara and Bridget

CONTENTS

INTRODUCTION

Self-defeating though it might be, we begin with an acknowledgement of the best book on Gaelic games ever written.

Not this one, but *Over the Bar* by Breandán Ó hEithir, which strikes the perfect balance: between exasperation at the insanity often tolerated, and sometimes celebrated, by the GAA, and the genuine affection one retains for wayward family members. Ó hEithir's clear-eyed view of the GAA's faults coexists with his acknowledgement of its grip on the country.

The views of the Aran Island native would be interesting to hear now, given the different tensions within the GAA. The push–pull of club and county, the challenge of competitive balance and demographic change. Rule changes and fixture scheduling vex administrators. Financial pressures coexist with the amateur status, not always to everyone's satisfaction. The media is a consideration. So is integration. So is redevelopment of stadiums.

Some or all of these issues existed in Ó hEithir's time, but lately they seem to be more interconnected than ever before. There are examples everywhere, but one will suffice.

Cork hosted Limerick in the second-last round of the 2024 Munster senior hurling championship. It was a massive game, with Cork teetering on the edge of elimination and Limerick keen to push them over the edge. Originally the game was meant to be played on a Sunday afternoon but it had to be moved to Saturday evening in order to facilitate preparing Páirc

Uí Chaoimh for a concert; the Cork County Board was not in a position to turn the concert down, given the size of the overrun on the redevelopment of the stadium. As a result of that move the game could not be shown on RTÉ and was moved to GAAGO, which led to a storm of criticism of that platform's joint owners, RTÉ and the GAA. Here were the component parts of the GAA intersecting: servicing the stadium debt meant a concert had to be accommodated, which meant the media coverage was rearranged, which led to a blazing fire of criticism. Ó hEithir would have enjoyed that one.

It hardly matters that many of the players and incidents he described in his book are now vanishingly remote from our own time. Ó hEithir was at games in the 1940s, which might as well have been played out between the Fir Bolg for all we recall of them, but his anatomy of the personalities and prejudices, motivations and mercenary impulses, is timeless. *Over the Bar* is also one of the funniest books ever written about Ireland. If you can complete the story that starts off with a lone drinker saying 'Ballindooley my bollocks' without laughing you may need to check for your own pulse.

To me, the book's strength is derived from two linked elements. Ó hEithir's subtitle tells you everything: *A Personal Relationship with the GAA*. Growing up on the Aran Islands at a time when radio was in its infancy, he came relatively late to the games and maintained a certain distance, which informs his view of the GAA. That leads in turn to his view of the organisation's strengths and weaknesses. The Ó hEithir perspective on how certain teams and individuals were blackguarded out of games, for instance, is an astringent corrective to the 'glory of the Gael' histories, and a couple of counties not lacking in self-regard get a hefty dunt or two along the way.

This is what sets the book apart. By stressing its perspective as his own personal view, Ó hEithir was able to criticise the GAA's hypocrisies, big and small, and isolate potential weaknesses. Along the way he pays due tribute to the organisation's achievements but without falling into sentimentality; to paraphrase a man fonder of rugby than Gaelic games, by looking into his own heart Ó hEithir found the best way to analyse the GAA. Everyone has a particular and personal relationship with the organisation, each of them valid and not all of them rational.

And that crystallises in Ó hEithir's account of a rugby game, not a hurling or football match. At the 1968 Ireland–Wales international the Irish forward Noel Murphy was struck by the Welsh player Brian Price, and Ó hEithir was surprised by the reaction of Murphy's teammates or rather their lack of reaction: 'I said to myself, there are the hard men! Now, if you were the Crusheen, Rathnew, or Buffers Alley hurlers . . .'

As an articulation of being unable to escape one's roots despite the impulse to broaden one's horizons it's difficult to beat. And all the more convincing in the light of Ó hEithir's brisk scepticism all through the book up to that point. In retrospect it's no surprise that two years later he wrote the greatest book about Irish politics, *The Begrudger's Guide to Irish Politics*, but that's another day's work.

In writing this book I didn't try to emulate Ó hEithir so much as to take his attitude as an example, because a lightly exasperated affection will be recognisable to many people who regard themselves as 'GAA people'. The best parallel may be a family dynamic; one can despair of a close relative's many faults, but woe betide the outsider who dares lodge a criticism of the same person. The GAA's intrinsic power – the way it grips people and how those people never really escape that grip – is a given in *Over the Bar*, and it remains as potent now as it was in the 1980s. Or the 1880s, come to that.

What I want to ask in this book is a simple question, which emanates from the GAA's position in Irish life. Where is it going?

To answer that I found myself asking the contributors some combination of the same questions. Is the GAA a delivery system for elite sport at inter-county level? Is it a participation movement which enables clubs all over Ireland to get people – especially kids – to play the game? Is it a real estate company managing and operating thousands of premises? Is it a media company working with and competing against other media companies?

Is it all these things? Can it be? Or do some of those strands contradict each other? And where does integration with ladies' football and camogie fit into all of that? All sorts of broader challenges confront the GAA too. Just as Ireland itself has issues with housing, climate change, demographics and a thousand other thorny corners of modern life, so does the GAA.

For a long time, the working title of this book came from a familiar refrain heard at my club's annual general meeting over the years: where are we going? It's applicable in the specific – what are we doing this year, with this captain, with this approach, with these players, with this coach? – and in the general.

Where are we going?

When I started I thought the 'going' part was the significant element, which is why I asked contributors about the ramifications of particular events – the GAAGO controversy, say, or the huge debt hanging over Páirc Uí Chaoimh. Their significance for the organisation at large, and the country as a whole, seemed the important element to focus on.

Now I'm not so sure. After a lot of talking to people with a lot to say, the 'we' part of that sentence became more and more central to everything. Because if I learned anything at all, it's that this is more than a game.

PART 1
ADAPTING

THE TWO (AT LEAST) GAAS

I started by chatting to Tom Ryan, Ard Stiúrthóir (director general) of the GAA, who didn't blink at the prospect of some fundamental questions, and there are few as fundamental as the most obvious of all: What is the GAA for?

My opener with interview subjects was to offer them a choice. Is the GAA a delivery system for elite sport at inter-county level, or is it a mass participation movement? Is it a real estate undertaking that manages and maintains stadiums and club grounds all over Ireland or a media company dealing with GAA+, RTÉ, TG4, online and print outlets, radio stations? All of those? Some of them?

To give Tom Ryan his due, he got to first principles pretty fast.

'I'm sure there were the same existential issues in the past. I can only imagine the period of independence and the Civil War or the Emergency. The Troubles was another challenging time. There's always something external to the GAA that is a "threat" but then you look at the calibre of the people and the strength of the movement and the good will that there is behind it and the heritage. We've been able to thrive in adversity in the past and we will again because of all those people, working in clubs that just get on with it.

'So it might look different. It might be played a bit differently. It might be played in different places and might be played by different people, but as long as it's recognisable as the GAA that's enough for me.'

Ryan's pragmatism on the GAA's essence was a reasonable foreshadowing of what many contributors thought. An element of adapting and changing without bending it out of all recognition can be found at all levels of the GAA, and he pointed to a concrete example in the way clubs adapt to different challenges and circumstances; sometimes by amalgamating clubs. That can be seen as a defeat in some eyes, but as we'll see later in this book, that's not always true.

'It's a really increasing phenomenon; you see it a lot in terms of whether it's the clubs formally amalgamating or whether we haven't enough on our under-sixteen team this year, so we'll fall in with the neighbours. It's to people's credit that they're responding to circumstances. As an organisation, we need to: number one, be more open to that and make it easier to happen and number two, to change our thinking in terms of how things are structured – that that maybe becomes more accepted. The reason you'd be worried about that is actually the whole thing is to do with where you're from. I don't want to see a Carlow team made up of people from outside the county, for instance.

'One of the great strengths we have is that a club is a solid thing. A GAA club is not easy to set up, which is maybe a bit of an impediment, but once it's there it's a solid thing. Other sports maybe have a different model, and it works for them in terms of being more easy to get together to play something with your friends; the downside of that is, maybe it's a bit more transient.

'It's something to look at, though – if you don't have enough people in your club to make up a team or if you're not on the team or even if you just want to play with a few other people, that could be another use for these centres of excellence. To put on a programme two or three nights a week, for particular age groups but irrespective of clubs, so people could fall in for a game. That kind of thing has a value to it in keeping people involved.

Whether it keeps people involved or stands on its own without the competitive, I'm not so sure.'

Ryan's flexibility surprised me. The perception of the GAA as a monolithic bastion of conservatism is a tired one in any case, but the head official praising different forms of participation and advocating fluid club memberships?

He didn't stop there.

'We characterise things as parish rules, for instance, which have less to do with church boundaries as much as that's how we define who we are. Parish rules have stood us in good stead for a hundred and forty, a hundred and fifty years, but the future of the country is going to look very different.

'Does that model of a GAA fit? Woe betide anybody that tampers with any of that stuff, but we need to be thinking about it and not in the context of playing strength or fighting other counties. It's in the context of sustainability: you look at your county structures. Is that the right way to be structured? You look at championship structures within counties – are they structured the right way? You look at the means by which fifteen people can come together to play, to represent something. Do they need to be bound by geographical boundaries that are rooted in the sixteenth century?

'Look, does it even have to be fifteen people?'

When Ryan mentioned fundamentals, he wasn't kidding. Even that relatively throwaway comment about the number of players on a hurling or football team brings us up against the basic principles of the GAA pretty fast. Readers will be familiar with various 13-a-side competitions around the country, particularly in areas with demographic challenges, but reducing the number of players from 15 would be a huge step for the GAA to consider. To take the playing side alone, it would open up new tactical challenges and developments; it wouldn't be an overstatement to say the sports would change completely overnight. For the man who runs the GAA to suggest that change is staggering.

'I think we need to be thinking along those lines. If the country is going to be different maybe we need to be different as well.

'I don't know if we're really ready for that, and you wouldn't like to get to the stage where a crisis means that we need to change things, to actually be able to respond. I think there will always be a cohort of people that want to play Gaelic and hurling. There are clubs all over the country which are fantastic resources; they take on the identity or they personify the locality. It's the de facto social community, public hub, which in some ways is a big burden for them to bear. But there's also a reassurance in that people know, whatever else happens, that that's going to be there.'

Burden and reassurance. It could be a motto for the GAA. But which GAA?

* * *

Ideally those contributing to this book would have had hard positions on the questions I raised in the introduction, perhaps saying the GAA is definitely about the action on the inter-county stage; or complaining that its property portfolio is so vast that it needs to be minded carefully at the expense of everything else. Some unambiguous statement of fact would be of huge benefit (to an author, anyway). A stark declaration of the GAA's focus would have set up some handy binaries, plenty of contradictions, duelling perspectives.

The reality was far less straightforward, of course. Elsewhere in this book a contributor picks out the GAA's ability to exist in ambiguity as a significant advantage for the organisation. Distilling down what the GAA is – its fundamental focus – certainly proved that.

For instance, Ryan came down firmly on the side of participation.

'It's the best thing about the GAA in a lot of ways. We use this term all the time, how we're unique. We're not really unique in a lot of respects, but that is one of the things that is special about it. Whether it's tennis or soccer or whatever, participation is the lifeblood of those too, but I'd like to think anyway that [GAA participation] does get a profile and a primacy in terms of people's thinking. The number of eight-year-olds that are playing hurling around the country, that's something we do take pride in.

'And it should drive the decisions that we're making. Now, it doesn't all the time, I know that, I know other things from time to time can take precedence, but if you're talking about what you want it to be like in fifty years – and that's the bit that is worthy of protection, worthy of promotion – then that's the bit that really does define the state of the organisation's health.

'And it isn't – though I might regret saying this – about the number of people that are watching the All-Ireland final. It's not the number of countries that the game is played in. It's the youngsters. That's a trite thing to say, but it is the truth that they are the people that will be playing senior club hurling in fifteen years' time, they are the people that you hope will be taking teams in thirty years' time and will be county chairperson, club secretaries. There's an organic aspect to that which I'm not sure applies in other codes or sports. With some the sense that you get that there are key families or maybe key geographic areas that perpetuate them. With ours we're very fortunate we have something far bigger, and that's the bit to protect.

'If you were to talk about primacy – and anytime you do that you run the risk of offending somebody – the bit that sets the pulse racing and the bit that you're getting excited about is, say, Patrick Horgan coming on to get a point for Cork, and that's great. But the bit that's serious for the future of the GAA is the participation element. And commercially that's the bit that is of interest to people. Obviously not every team is going to be at the business end of the championship, so not every county, when they're going looking for sponsorship, can say to a business, "Well, you know, there's a good chance we'll be organising a homecoming in conjunction with yourselves at the end of the championship." In fact, most counties can't do that. But a lot of commercial enterprises are not really that interested in that anyway; it's nice to have, but it's the impact in communities, that community reach and profile, and the positive aspects of all of that which is attraction to companies now.

'I know that also kind of runs the risk of undermining it a little bit when you make those associations, but it is fair to say that there's a value far beyond the commercial. I mention that in the sense that it's interesting to see that other people with maybe a different perspective from ourselves, or different things that are driving them from ourselves, see the value in that.'

Ryan's points were well made, and he didn't shy away from taking a position. Flying the flag for participation as the GAA's bottom line was unambiguous, and he made a good argument that other elements of the Association's mission flow from that.

Tom Parsons, CEO of the Gaelic Players Association (GPA), also gave his view on priorities in the GAA. By representing inter-county players the GPA has often been a lightning rod for criticism within the GAA, to put it politely. Its fiercest critics see it as undermining the GAA's ethos by separating elite players from the rest of the GAA and absorbing too many of the GAA's resources in funding schemes. The GPA counter-argument – which Parsons articulates elsewhere in this book – is that the inter-county game generates the funding and inter-county players deserve the best support in doing so.

Parsons started by saying that there are 'two lines of organisation in the GAA that do two very different things for the most part'.

'For a long time everything was merged into one but I think now we see two different realities, nearly a two-tier GAA. The first – I've seen it first hand – is the heartbeat of the GAA, the 2,200 clubs. What's unique about Ireland, it's protecting small towns, keeping kids in small towns . . . I've seen that myself in Charlestown. A clubmate of mine died and the town got together and the local club raised nearly one million euro in his name, built facilities, the pitch is in his name and kids can go there. I've seen that, whether it's my parents doing the club lotto, people fundraising, the club players coaching kids. You can't measure the impact and it's grounded in voluntarism, in community spirit, it's not just sport. If you don't play you can join a committee, if a kid gets sick a GoFundMe page is started, all of that. For the most part that's self-sufficient. I know there are the odd applications for capital grants and so on, but for the most part it drives itself, it's very special. People are treated equally; that community, it's fantastic.'

And the second?

'The other part of the GAA, which I'm in the middle of, is the inter-county piece, and in a lot of people's eyes, who may see the good in the GAA, they see the inter-county part as a problem child. It doesn't have the same feel of voluntarism. Take All-Ireland final day, which has 82,000 people paying a minimum of a hundred euro each, and in the run-up to that tickets are used by many clubs for fundraising so people can end up paying, indirectly, up to a thousand. Programmes cost money, players have jerseys with three different sponsors, it's broadcast around the world – this is serious business, and it's special as well. This is the best of our club players representing the county, and it's still amateur, there's a lot of voluntarism going on as well – but it's also different.

'And this is where the human spirit kicks in. We're not designed to slow down but to get better, to improve, to get bigger and faster. Everything evolves, right down to your smartphone. It's very hard to stop that and say, "We need to go backwards." That's true of sport, where there're new ways to do things, new ways to train, to improve facilities, to market the games better. The curve is always going one way. And I know these are questions rather than solutions, but you have to ask about the inter-county game, whether it's a different type of amateurism and of voluntarism. There's a huge amount of professionalism needed to run that, and that won't be pulled back either. If that were pulled back the sports might never leave the island – they might not achieve the status of Olympic sports, for instance, while the GAA units serving the diaspora might not reach their potential.

'Those are questions we need to ask – where does it go?'

Parsons teased that out further with reference to reality and revenue.

'Where it has gone already, year on year we have huge spending on inter-county teams. Largely every manager and backroom team are all paid. There's a handful of volunteers. There are 152 staff paid centrally who are paid in the realm of thirteen million annually according to the GAA's accounts – all professional people in financial, marketing, IT and commercial roles. They're in their roles to do better, to find better ways of doing their jobs in facilitating the GAA.

'At county level you're looking at organisations with P and L (profit and loss) of two million, three million per year. The county chair is a voluntary position but some counties now have professional CEOs, and to do this right – to be compliant – that's needed. When the GAA does its economic report on the amounts generated by county, provincial and central means it equates to 254 million. That's very big business and it doesn't even take into consideration the club piece.

'What the GPA is grappling with as a player representative body is that these players are in both worlds. For half the year they're involved in voluntarism, the local club, being local volunteers and coaching sessions themselves, being the face of the club for fundraising – voluntarism to the core. For the other half of the year you're still an amateur and a volunteer but you're also asking, "Hold on, is everybody a volunteer here the way everyone in my club is a volunteer?" And that may not be the case at inter-county level. At the club level a coach may be someone's dad, but at inter-county the coach is more likely to be a seasoned campaigner who's well compensated. Food after training at inter-county isn't ham sandwiches being pulled together by the parents in the club but a catering company – professionals again.

'The players are looking at that. And they're saying, "Of course we want to be amateurs," but they're also asking why, in this two-tier system, so many people are professionals but players are amateurs and at a cost? To be an amateur anything there's a cost. Of course there is. If you take up tennis tomorrow you have to buy the racquet, lessons, membership – of course it's going to cost you. What players are grappling with now is whether it should cost them to be in tier one – and of course it should, because we're all volunteers – and tier two, where they're not so sure it should cost them. The system for a lot of people in tier two is not one that costs them but actually provides them with a career and a profession. We're at a stage now where players in tier two are saying, "Of course I'll be amateur but I need to be well looked after and not at a cost."'

The proof of that is in the experience of inter-county players, he added.

'For instance, if a player on an inter-county panel is a student, playing in Croke Park or wherever on a Sunday, there's not a hope in hell he can hold down a bar job on a Saturday night for pocket money. So a student bursary needs to be designed so he's not at a cost.

'If the government recognises professional sportspeople with tax breaks, the economic return of these games needs to be recognised. That means recognising the referees, the county board chairman, as well.

'How do we look after the two-tier system without it being exploitative? If we don't do that, we can't continue with more sponsors on the jerseys or raising ticket prices. Every year the revenue increases but so do the demands of an elite game. We need to look at how we increase the value proposition here and make sure it doesn't cost players. Particularly when the next generation of players might not be the same stoics we've seen in the last few decades. Who mightn't be willing to forego the weekend work as a student to play for the county. We might not see the old twelve-year commitment of a player to the county team, and more of a continued churn of players; we might lose the role model aspect of the games. So we're at a delicate stage in terms of that balance.

'Can we roll it back? Back to the ticket prices of the early noughties, to straight knock-out, to the time before video analysis? I doubt it. The sponsors and commercial partners aren't going to back that. Neither are costs such as stadium maintenance. So we modernise it, recognise that a large part of tier two is big business, recognise amateurism but accept that what applied in the eighties and nineties won't work in the 2040s, for instance.

'Amateurism is not dying at the club level. Not at all. But at inter-county level it's dying.'

What's interesting is that both Toms, Ryan and Parsons, acknowledge the amount of moving parts involved in the GAA. Ryan stressed the importance of participation but pointed to the attractions of the inter-county game; he freely admitted that other things take precedence at times, a simple statement of fact. Parsons' focus on the inter-county game was understandable, given his role as head of the GPA (and there are plenty of GAA people with a reflexive dislike of the player organisation on the grounds of elitism). But the former Mayo footballer began by stressing the importance of the club ethos and delineated its significance precisely. Again, a statement of fact.

Interestingly, some other comments from the two men reverberate elsewhere in this book. When Tom Ryan mentions the commercial attraction of the game being linked to what it stands for, that's an idea that gets teased out when discussing Páirc Uí Chaoimh's sponsorship travails.

Tom Parsons' comments on the level of interest future inter-county players may have in the game finds an echo in Dara Ó Cinnéide's thoughts on the meaning of representing one's county.

Parsons' aside about management teams – that most of them are paid – may be the best segue to discussing one of the greatest hypocrisies in Irish life, never mind the GAA or even sport on this island. How are managers being paid secretly in a game that proclaims its amateurism and volunteer ethos so loudly? Well, we'll come to that.

First, though, why is the support so poor for people who should be paid well for what they do for the GAA?

STOP, STOP, STOP ASKING FORMER COUNTY PLAYERS TO REFEREE

It never ends for referees.

In hurling, even as this book was being written, the Cork County Board was protesting ever so loudly that it had no issue with how referee Johnny Murphy had handled the All-Ireland senior hurling final. But it also acknowledged that it had sought clarity from him after the game about an incident that had occurred on the field of play. And Gaelic football referees were juggling with an array of new demands introduced by the Football Review Committee's tinkering with Gaelic football rules.

When I spoke to Barry Kelly, one of the most experienced GAA officials around, I asked where he thought Gaelic games refereeing was in general. He soon got specific.

'I read Owen Doyle, the rugby referee, this year commenting on the quality of rugby refereeing, and he was saying there are good refs in Ireland and good refs in South Africa, but they can't take Ireland–South Africa games, so then you're looking at other countries' refs and wondering how good are they . . .

'I don't think we're a million miles from that scenario insofar as in inter-county hurling, say, there may be twelve referees on the championship panel but six or seven may not have a huge amount of experience or may not be eligible for a game, depending on which counties are playing. And some of those may not even be involved in five years' time anyway. It's a similar situation in football, where there has been great service given by the likes of David Coldrick and Joe McQuillan and a few more, so I would be concerned.

'In Leinster in particular there is a dearth of young referees coming through to push on to the next level, lads in their mid- to late twenties. Because that's what you need to do, really, to almost sacrifice the playing career for refereeing. Take Leinster as an example. You break through from the club to the provincial refereeing panel, maybe four or five years on the Leinster panel then before you break through to the national panel. If you're to get ten years out of a referee on the national panel then he's got to be there at thirty-four, thirty-five years of age, maybe – and to do that he's got to have ten years' refereeing behind him at least. So where do you fit playing in around that?'

Support for referees is vital and could be improved, he added.

'As far as I can see there are two people employed full time in Croke Park looking after this [refereeing] but I've seen references to 350 GAA coaches being employed. That means millions are being spent on coaching, which I obviously don't have a problem with, but in a way you really need to be employing referees, even on a part-time basis.

And employing support for them. Say a referee has a tough day – he makes some controversial calls and there's a lot of focus on him. There should be someone employed by the GAA who can say, "Hey, Johnny, I'll be in your neck of the woods this week and I'll bring you to lunch and we'll have a chat about the game. We'll work through it and discuss it." It doesn't need huge money – you could have someone retained on twenty grand a year part time to do that.'

Looping back to getting people involved as referees, the usual line is 'we need more former players taking up the whistle', but Kelly isn't long-skewering that notion. There was a time in the fifties when Peter McDermott might be lining out in an

All-Ireland for Meath and refereeing an All-Ireland final a year or two later, but those days are long gone.

'That thinking fails to account for the reality, really. Imagine going up to a player after he's finished up, at maybe thirty-three or thirty-four years of age. At that stage he has probably been involved in serious sport for twenty years with underage, schools, colleges, club and inter-county. At that point in his life he's probably in a serious relationship, possibly with a couple of kids, and his work situation may be progressing to a stage where he has more commitments and responsibilities. Imagine that player turning around to his partner or wife and saying, "I'm going to throw my hat in the ring as a referee now. There's a fair bit of commitment involved."

'And there is. Two-hour journeys, games, bite to eat – you could be gone eleven hours, so the idea of the former players taking up the cudgels . . . I don't see it happening because in fairness, they've given their service to the GAA.'

That leads to counties getting creative in enticing people to take up the whistle.

'In Westmeath we run refereeing courses and every year there are the same exhortations to clubs, "We need referees" and so on. I'm the Westmeath minor board chairman and last year we almost coerced clubs that are at under-twelve level: we said, "If you don't supply a referee at under-twelve level you don't get home games under twelve."

'So we had about seventy-five guys that did the course but it was an unnatural figure, thirty-three of them have actively taken a match so far. Most did the course to get around the issue we presented – though on the other hand we did have thirty-three referee a game, which is great. Still, how many of them will continue? We had to use a stick and carrot approach, and it was mostly stick.'

Should Croke Park be following that approach?

'Some counties are going down the road of a punitive approach in the sense that [if] your club doesn't apply referees, then you don't get All-Ireland final tickets, or you might get fined, or you might not get home games. It's probably a strength of the Association that there's a reluctance to impose financial penalties, because who's going to pay that? It comes out of the lotto account and it's hard enough to raise money in the GAA. Clubs are under pressure as well.'

Is this all a bit of a catch-22? If referees were paid just a little more, would it just make it just a little more attractive? The GAA's amateur ethos is laudable, but facilitating more referees would surely help?

'A Westmeath referee for an adult club match gets fifty euro. Would more money make it more attractive? It's a touchy one. Yes, there are a lot of referees whose primary motivation is the money, and then there are the guys who enjoy it and the money is kind of almost secondary. And there are other factors. Westmeath is a small county so you're never travelling that far. If I went from Athlone to Mullingar for a game, which would be rare, it's thirty miles. It's a lot different in counties like Cork and Galway and Donegal.

'At county level it's different. At club level the fee isn't based on mileage – if it was I'd get nothing half the time because I rarely travel more than five miles to a game. At county level it's just your mileage and an allowance for a bite to eat. And that's become very stringent, whereas before it was more relaxed.

'Recently enough I was at a club match and the referee was there a good forty-five minutes before the start so he was gone a good four hours from home – he had a fifty-mile round trip. The meal allowance is €13.70, so if he made a full claim he'd have had about forty-four euro. But if he'd refereed a local club game he'd have had fifty. At inter-county level a referee could be gone ten or eleven hours, wear and tear on the car, all of that – his umpires are getting absolutely nothing, only a meal – so after everything there's very little financial reward. The point being, he'd also be better off financially handling a local game, if finance is the motivation. And if you suddenly increased the referees allowance to ninety-five cent a mile the GPA would be hot on your heels as well.'

This is a point worth noting, of course. The GAA is no more a monolith marching together in lockstep than any other mass movement. There are plenty of sectoral interests keeping a close eye on funding allocations and budgetary commitments; in fact, the GPA might not be the only interested party when it comes to increased mileage rates.

On top of the financial consideration, the time commitment is hugely significant, Kelly pointed out. Driving to and from a game is only the start.

'Take a national league weekend with double fixtures, football and hurling. There's a sending-off in a football game and that county is going to want that player available for the next weekend. There's no doubt that they're going to appeal, so for the lads in Croke Park who have to deal with that appeal, it's almost like preparing a court case; there's a huge amount of i's to be dotted and t's to be crossed and video evidence. You can't just go in; you have to make sure your case is prepared properly. It's hugely time-consuming, and obviously there might be more than one appeal arising out of each weekend. All of that is alongside the appeals meetings themselves and seminars on rules and committee meetings on those appeals and seminars. Fellas like Donal Smith [GAA National Match Officials Coordinator] are at those meetings at Croke Park every weekend of games.'

There are other complications. Hawk-Eye means there are two different sets of rules for inter-county games, those with the technology available and those without.

'There was a game last summer [2023] in Hyde Park with a very tough call, a Mayo 45 that replays showed came off a Mayo player. Colm Reape kicked the 45 and it could have been the difference between winning and losing the game. But there's no Hawk-Eye in Hyde Park. The big hurling matches tend to have it because they're in Thurles and Croke Park, but I'd be a traditionalist in the sense that – as we've seen across the water in England with VAR – has it improved things?'

Not according to Gary Lineker et al., as *Match of the Day* fans can attest. Kelly finesses the point, however, with the example of a different sport and brings up the spectre of refereeing to video confirmation rather than officiating to the official's own judgement.

'In rugby – and I'm not anti-rugby at all when I say this – it seems that unless the guy gets the ball and dots it down under the posts the referee tends to automatically go to the TV to confirm the score. The average rugby game basically lasts two hours because you have all these stoppages. I'm not entirely sure about technology in this sense. People talk about managers having the ability to challenge one decision or two, but even bringing that into inter-county senior football and hurling would still require a fair degree of technology to be imple-mented. You'd have to bring it into Clones and Letterkenny and Páirc Uí Rinn, all of these places. I'm not saying we should opt for the lesser option but sometimes we look directly across at soccer without taking on board that that is a global game. The figures bandied about in English soccer, in terms of tele-vision deals and attendances and club earnings and so on, those are getting into the billions. It's different.

'Sometimes we're comparing ourselves to a global game played by every country in the world – every young child that has ever walked and played soccer amounts, eventually, to billions of people who've played or been involved with the game. Ours is very much an Irish game – it's played by lots of people here, the diaspora enjoy it, which is great to see, but it's still very much a local, national game.'

Which is not to say it's immune to change. Kelly has seen the benefits of rule changes and also the way those changes can influence the very skills of the game.

'I think changes like the square ball rule in football have been a godsend in that there are very few mistakes made. Absolutely. I was at a sandbox game [trialling] for the new football rules [and] what was interesting was the lack of two-point shots in the game, shots from forty metres. The reason was, as players pointed out, they don't practise that skill. They're playing one way the whole time where you hold possession until you get close enough for a shot – closer than forty metres.

'If you take a shot from that distance and you don't score, then at half-time that's [put] down as you [losing] possession. But if you made a five-yard handpass, then it's a positive outcome when the stats are examined. In football you don't take a shot unless your best forward is twenty-five yards out on the D and he's free.

'It's funny because in hurling [Limerick manager] John Kiely seems to work to the opposite plan – his players shoot all the time. In one game last year they got off fifty-one shots, and clearly if they have a success rate of sixty-six per cent they'll outscore the opponents; and hitting the ball wide isn't necessarily a turnover. They're confident that they have a very good chance of winning the ball again from the opposing puck-out, whereas in football giving the ball away is a fear, because there's a chance [that] if you lose the ball you may not see it again for three or four minutes.

'Two referees may not be needed in football because games are so lateral, but are two referees possible in hurling with numbers? You may not be able to have two refs for a club game, but if you have two refs at inter-county, or after the All-Ireland quarter-finals, then you have two different ways of refereeing. And that would ask very different questions of teams.'

FOR THE HONOUR OF THE LITTLE VILLAGE, AND THE ONE DOWN THE ROAD AS WELL

Amalgamation is a shadow that looms over many GAA clubs, particularly in rural Ireland.

When I wrote *GAAconomics* former President Nickey Brennan acknowledged that reality in the general and the specific; his club, Conahy Shamrocks, is one of the smaller outfits in Kilkenny. If it had to happen it had to happen, he said, adding that when and if it did he would probably weep for a week. That's an outlook many GAA members will recognise: the harsh reality that muscles its way past a vague formulation.

Dara Ó Cinnéide explained it from his perspective.

'We had our existential moment a few years back when Dingle, our bitterest rivals [Ó Cinnéide is a member of An Ghaeltacht], made a submission to us to see if we'd amalgamate with them at underage because they were struggling for numbers. There was a meeting called to discuss it but it had to be called off, so at mass the following Sunday someone said to me, "Would you show your face at that meeting because I have a feeling this thing is going to happen?" I went in to the meeting and there were over thirty people there, a lot of parents of talented footballers, and after listening to the discussions for about forty-five minutes I piped up.

'I said that the amalgamated teams would probably be good enough to win championships and medals, but that the whole point of the GAA was our corner forward, who would lose his place if we amalgamated with Dingle because he wouldn't be good enough for the first fifteen. Even if we won a cup we could lose players like him because he would think, "They don't value me, so why would I bother playing?"'

Ó Cinnéide went deeper:

'Our mistake as a club for years was to say, "We have Darragh Ó Sé playing for Kerry, Dara Ó Cinnéide playing for Kerry, we've won this and that." That was never the success of it. I felt a much better spirit in the club in the early nineties when we were a division three novice team.

'Eventually two of us convinced thirty-odd people at the meeting not to amalgamate, but of course I then had to go back to Dingle to tell them it was off – I was the blackest of the black Gaeltacht men, the man who blocked it all. I had to go to Diarmuid Murphy, Breandan Fitz, lads I knew well, and I told them this wasn't an anti-Dingle thing, it was a pro-Gaeltacht, pro-GAA thing. It's not that you're not welcome, I just don't think it's the right thing for our club. The word "club" even suggests cliquish and clannish, and I want that borderline hatred, that rivalry, to continue. I felt that that would disappear if we amalgamated. Part of my raison d'être would vanish overnight.

'That was an existential crisis for the two clubs because they were struggling for numbers, while for us . . . I asked one of our coaches if we had the numbers to field a team in the grade, and he said we had. My point was that surely it was our mission to get every Tom, Dick and Harry – with two left feet if necessary – to play football, to wear the Gaeltacht jersey and to stand for something as opposed to just winning a medal.'

The key to the west Kerry experience may be in Ó Cinnéide's point about numbers. At the end of the day, An Ghaeltacht had them. But what happens when you don't have the numbers and you don't have an alternative?

Tom O'Flaherty of Churchtown in north Cork broke the process down for me. Churchtown isn't far from another village, Liscarroll: two houses, both alike in dignity, but Shakespeare couldn't have completed the quotation in good faith. The grudges weren't ancient. And there was no mutiny.

'The two clubs are from the same parish but were two separate clubs,' said O'Flaherty, a longtime Churchtown player and officer.

'Back in the day, forty years ago, Granard Gaels was born – that was when we didn't have enough or they didn't have enough to field an underage team. When we didn't have enough we'd amalgamate under that banner. Granard is a little townland on the border, so it was sort of fifty–fifty in terms of location.

'Around fifteen to seventeen years ago there wasn't enough on either side for a team, though, and it was clear it wasn't just one year, that it was going to continue. The Granard Gaels idea came back in then for another sustained period, and that needed to survive long enough for the kids to get involved, and the crop we had were handy enough, one of them being Colin O'Brien, who's been on the Cork senior hurling squad.'

It was the watershed moment. Numbers were becoming an insurmountable struggle for each club on their own, and the fact that they were both looking at a talented crop between the two clubs made action non-negotiable. Join or die. Or at least miss out on some very good players.

'One crowd approached the other. I don't know whether the conversation started in a pub or over the phone or whatever, but the numbers weren't getting any stronger and we could all see these boys were coming and they were going well, they were playing Premier Minor grade, for example. And they weren't going to split up again as adults, it just made no sense. So it sort of graduated from that point. There was a kind of halfway house then, when Liscarroll said, "Look, we'll do the football team only if you'll [Churchtown] do the hurling team only."

'It had been going well prior to that for the two clubs but fellas were getting too old and then there was a stage where neither crowd were going very well and numbers was an issue, probably the big issue. That was that.'

Each club transferred all its players across the border to Churchtown for hurling or to Liscarroll for football, and then around that time the youngsters, who had only ever played together, were coming up to junior.

'They were never going to want to split because they knew no different. Growing up, we had stayed local in Churchtown and only knew lads from Churchtown. The same in Liscarroll. Now they can go to secondary school in Mallow or Buttevant or Charleville. I never really knew the lads from Liscarroll, we just played against them. The new cohort were different; they all knew each other.'

Presumably, however, there were a couple of diehards in both places – the type to put the foot down and say, 'No, we'll keep our jersey, our crest, our field'?

'And that's okay too, because it was important to them,' said O'Flaherty. 'But they were at the other end of the spectrum. Eventually someone said, "Are we doing this or are we not?"'

There were advantages the clubs enjoyed, small matters that became easy wins:

'Churchtown were green and gold and Liscarroll were green and white, so the jersey became green, white and gold and no one lost anything. Fellas were looking at that, in fact, and were thinking, "We could have a class jersey like that." Now if we were black and white and they were green and gold, small things like that could count. But we got a nice green white and gold jersey and then it got down to, "Are we doing this top to bottom, now?"

'The only bone of contention was initially someone said, "Alright, the juvenile club is called Granard Gaels, would we call the adult club the same?" But a lot of people on both sides said, "No, we'll call it Liscarroll-Churchtown or Churchtown-Liscarroll, we'll decide later." People wanted to keep their names, to keep their colour – that stuff was very important.'

More important than other stuff, as it turned out. The two club committees met and O'Flaherty said there were no objections about who was going to be chairman and who was going to be treasurer:

'It was, "Okay, we'll toss a coin, you get the first chair and we get the first secretary, and so on." It was just sorting out those small teething problems. The existing treasurers came forward as co-treasurers so nobody could doubt that everyone was participating. You want everyone to stay around at the start, kind of like if a company is bought out.

'Diarmuid O'Donovan with the Cork County Board was very knowledgeable and a big help. The vote was on the first of March 2016 and you had to be a member to vote. People like my father, God rest him, born right on the border between the two and who would have had family on both sides, they all went back to their own camp and voted.'

The voting threw up a speed bump, though.

'In Liscarroll there was one against amalgamation, I think, but in Churchtown, I think there were seventy votes or seventy-five, but there were twenty rejections, so it failed. Then we were thinking, "What now?" It was a bit of a clusterf—, to be honest.'

O'Flaherty recalls 'a fairly open and honest conversation' to address the matter.

'There were a lot of fellas sitting around in a room saying, "But hang on, I thought that this or that would happen." I think a couple of old lads never realised that if it didn't go through we'd be out of competition for quite a few years – until the kids in the estates were big enough to play. And that's grand, we might have a load of eight-year-olds, but it meant we'd have no twelve-year-olds for a few years, and then in reality it would take ten years before we could actually be a club again.

'The bottom line was fellas started to change their minds in front of us, if you like, because they realised what the rejection meant. And that stung, too – that kind of rejection vote is seismic in a small country place.

'We had a good minor team coming, we'd have two pitches, good new jerseys and a chance to move up a bit. Not being kingpins by any means but a club with a realistic chance of getting to a junior county final and winning it. And it was that prospect or going back to getting forty-year-olds out to play until their own sons got old enough to play. It developed slowly, but the big thing was necessity.'

Then came the formalities. Both clubs had to make their case to the Cork County Board.

'The board had to have a chat amongst themselves to see were they going to allow this – you couldn't have the Barrs and the Rockies [Blackrock and St Finbarr's] joining, for example, and have one superclub and everyone else losing to them. There were a few times where both sets of us had to go to Páirc Uí Chaoimh to sit down and basically substantiate the arguments. And that's only right. You need to do that too, because you need due diligence in this stuff.

'Once that was done then they had instructions and procedures to follow. You need to confirm your home pitch, you need to confirm your name, your club jerseys, and all of this has to be approved by Páirc Uí Chaoimh.

'I don't think there was a tremendous amount of paperwork. You did have the two previous clubs ceasing to exist, you have to dissolve the two clubs, but GAA facilities in the country are vested in the GAA, so you can't have a situation where a chancer might come in and be appointed chairman so he could sell a pitch or whatever down the line.

'What that meant as well was looking at what might happen. If this amalgamation doesn't work out, will the other crowd take or half own our lovely facilities? Are we going to end up giving them money to clear off? When it's vested in the GAA, though, it can't be sold, and I think even the Uachtarán of the day couldn't sell the ground.

'If some fella said to me, "I'll buy your pitch and also build you different facilities with 5G pitches and so on halfway between both villages", I'd say no thanks. For me it's important that young lads and young girls can walk up to the field. We have a hurling wall, a two-sided wall, now, next to a playground, and it's a little centre to our little village. I could understand as well the point of view of someone saying, "What are we doing in Liscarroll? We're gonna protect it at all costs. If the next Christy Ring comes from Liscarroll he's wearing my club jersey."'

There were other factors. O'Flaherty points out that there was a lot of development in Churchtown going back to the early noughties, when what had been a small sleepy village suddenly had four housing estates, all of them full.

'Still, it took the guts of twenty years for us to see the fruits of those estates in terms of kids coming to the club. The houses were being built around 1998, 1999, when a local entrepreneur, Jerry Murphy, bought a field and said, "I'm going to bring this village back to life." I'd say people laughed at him back then, but it was probably the single biggest moment in the life of the village.

'If you look at other villages that were just like Churchtown then, they didn't get that much development. And now they're starting to look around. I know for a fact there are GAA clubs looking at us who might have been giggling at us a couple of years ago and now they're saying, "Feck it, maybe we should do it too."'

Churchtown surfed the boost given by the housing developments, and the pandemic brought another, less expected boost.

'Those houses were built maybe around 2000, and they sold very quickly. The builder couldn't get them up quick enough; other people spotted that, bought a field and did the same, and off it went. Now we have a hundred-odd boys between eight and eighteen, whereas before the national school wouldn't have had a hundred people in the building between teachers, girls and boys.

'There was a huge amount of people who would have moved in around here post-Covid. Pre-Covid I was working kind of up and down the country, where projects were going on, but now I'm at home three days a week. I know people here who moved down from Douglas in Cork city, they couldn't believe their luck with the price of houses. You can get to Cork city, Limerick city, up to Thurles or down to Killarney, all within an hour. We're only two miles off the main road, so we did get lucky in that way. If we were another five miles further back it mightn't be as handy.

'Those people were coming in, young married couples, they find there's a pub and a GAA club so they'll give it a go. They were coming in the door and they were welcomed with open arms and they're now coaches, officers, because they're in the place twenty years, they're shoving fifty, and their kids are playing. Now we see that boost.'

The dividend comes at the far side as well.

'The other side of that is someone like Colin O'Brien, a wonderful young player. In the old days everyone would be telling him to get out of our club and to go elsewhere if he wanted to play for Cork but the amalgamation meant he could show his ability here. Now we'd have lads coming to play football for us from Dromina; they play underage hurling with Shandrum, but there's no football played there so they come over to us because they'd see our facilities, a decent club and so on.

'Before the traffic went the other way, fellas were going to Clyda or wherever to play football. All of these small bits come together.'

In small places small things make a difference, but there can also be unintended consequences. In nearby Castlemagner 'someone built a crèche next to the national school and now it's overflowing,' says O'Flaherty.

'And now the national school is overflowing, and all those people are staying in Castlemagner. But another village nearby may not have a crèche, so when people say, "We have to drop our kids somewhere, well, his friends are over there, we'll drop him here," that leads to, "You should let your kids play sport with their friends." So those other villages may suffer then in terms of numbers if the kids are falling in with Castlemagner.

'Those are significant matters in small places. When we got those houses in Churchtown twenty-odd years ago it was monumental. It was absolutely huge. People realised there was a bit of life to Churchtown, it got bigger, the school has got bigger and so on. It's not perfect but there's life there anyway. There are cars there, people walking the street, there are shops, all of that. It all helps.'

The shared facilities are busy now, says O'Flaherty, in both places.

'When I was young, if your under-twelve team was out your under-sixteen team couldn't possibly be out because they had the same set of cars driving the players. Now we've started having a community training night. The nursery, ten- and twelve-year-olds, all train on the same field at the same time. That's building a bit of community spirit but at the same time it means that we get them all off the field after an hour and get the next crowd on. So we need two pitches.'

Particularly as another club also uses the facilities.

'St Mary's are a Liscarroll–Dromina ladies' football team and they have no facilities of their own. They would have leaned heavily on Liscarroll and Dromina back in the day, but since the amalgamation they use the Churchtown field more, or Dromina's. It all means that you have to book your slot really, because those fields are full all the time. There's room for everyone, there's great facilities in Churchtown – a big car park, there's a big field with a stand, there's a meeting room, dressing rooms, some indoor five-a-side areas with a viewing area for a few lads pucking around.

'If you had to pick one field we would have picked Churchtown, but there was never any question that we wouldn't keep Liscarroll as well. It was important to people, and we needed it. If this amalgamation were to happen somewhere else, up by Grenagh for example, someone might say, "Sell that field, it's worth a million quid," but we didn't have that problem.

'The next thing that has to happen is we have to get more land because when integration happens and St Mary's join us, then we'll need more space because everyone has to play.'

Selling one club's field might have seemed an obvious solution, but O'Flaherty disagrees:

'We were never going to sell [a pitch] because there were plenty of reasons to not sell and no good reasons to sell.

'First, if someone said, "I'll give you half a million for that field" or more, there would have been awful sadness on one side or the other. We had better facilities over in Churchtown, so it was never a question of selling that, but it could have been a situation then for the Liscarroll people of, "F— me, I can't even walk into my own village and watch a match?" That's their club, we're joining their club and I don't want to do that.

'In fairness, there's so many coaches criss-crossing that it's gone far beyond what fellas might have been thinking six months in: "How many of us and how many of them?"; "Would we have managed on our own?" That sort of nonsense is long gone.'

Amalgamation has been a success for Churchtown and Liscarroll. But O'Flaherty says that clubs considering the option need to consider the alternative as well.

'There's an awful lot of places with good, proper GAA clubs, with a hero putting out the flags every day of the week and selling the lotto tickets. There's one of those people in every club in every village. But everything they have done will die if they don't secure it. I could list ten villages off the top of my head, and I'd hate to not go out to them for matches any more. I'd hate not to see the green and gold of Ballyclough or some other club's colours, but are they going to get to a stage where they can only play twelve-a-side games?

'Clubs evolve. And people's involvement evolves. I was the secretary but my kids were small and I was married a couple of years, so after a while I said, "I've enough to do now, I need to stay at home and work." And I stepped back and wasn't seen at a match then for a while. Someone else did the job. There's a cycle to it. I'd have zero regrets on this. I don't think even the odd old stalwart would. Even lads who would remember a time when Churchtown and Liscarroll were big rivals, and who would have played and punched each other and everything else on the field, well, they're also getting to an age anyway where they're going to relax. At sixty you're not gonna punch a guy in the pub. All of that stuff evolves anyway and now they're dyed-in-the-wool green, white and gold men.

'The things you're worried about, the things which may be problems . . . what you do know that in a couple of years your club will be thriving so when your kid is big enough to play, and your buddy's kid is going to be big enough to play, off they'll go to play just like you and your buddy did in your time.

'It's positive only for me, and I know I'm not alone in that. We had fellas playing Sigerson, the Fitzgibbon Cup captain, a dual Cork minor, someone on the Cork under-twenty extended squad last year . . . Would all of that have happened if we didn't amalgamate? I don't think it would. So it's a success at that end too. If I were asked by someone who was thinking about amalgamation for his club, I'd say, "Absolutely, do it." Because the stuff that you're worried about, it's more than likely that that won't happen and you'll avoid a negative cycle. Also, if you're thinking of it then make the jump. Because otherwise you'll be years behind other clubs when they do it.'

Not every club is in this position, of course. A lot of factors came together to help Churchtown and Liscarroll, and the dividend is visible in facilities, inter-county players, integration.

But the great selling point about amalgamation is participation. If the GAA is serious about participation – and it is – affording kids the opportunity to play the games is the motivation that should trump everything.

DEMOGRAPHICS CAN BE CHALLENGING ANYWHERE

Over a century ago the power in Cork hurling was centred on a few streets overlooking the South Channel of the River Lee. Redmonds drew from a small, close-knit community around Barrack Street to win five county titles. They were the power in the land and provided plenty of players to Cork senior teams; going back to the time when club sides represented counties, in fact, they collected an All-Ireland title themselves in 1892.

One hundred years later Redmonds were struggling to survive. Students and other transient residents had replaced the large families who traditionally stocked their teams and the club weren't harvesting new players from freshly built apartments. A change in the area's population profile was killing the old Sporting Reds as the population of Cork moved out and away from the city centre.

It's not depopulation in the classic sense, of course. There are thousands of people living in the centre of Cork city, just as there are in other cities and towns around the country. The inevitable time-lag between people moving to inner cities and having the children who will fill out under-ten teams can be fatal for old clubs like Redmonds, but that is a challenge that many rural clubs would welcome. We'll see later in this book that there are swathes of Ireland the size of a county that struggle to produce one team at under-seventeen level (and playing 13-a-side at that).

But some urban areas face challenges all their own. Late in 2023 the relegation of Glen Rovers from Cork club hurling's top tier was a headline event in the county. It also came with a wider context, one with elements as disparate as demographic change and hostile infrastructure, all glazed with institutional indifference.

The Glen's relegation is part of a marked decline. Twenty years ago the northside of Cork city, a Gaelic games heartland for decades, had three senior hurling teams and two senior football teams. With the demotion of the Glen it had none at all.

Why?

Parking the sports-specific issues involved for a moment, the demographic challenges offered a good starting point. They were slightly different from those faced by Redmonds. Denis Coughlan, a legendary figure in Glen Rovers, and the GAA as a whole, pointed out the week his club was relegated that it was short on manpower, like others on the northside of Cork.

Always an astute observer, Coughlan told the *Examiner* that a lack of new housing hurt clubs north of the river:

> You look at the southside city clubs, the likes of Douglas, Blackrock, Nemo, Barrs, and Bishopstown, they have much more access to private housing and land to build on, and then encourage people to come in and stay in the city, as opposed to the northside as we see it now. So I think it is the lack of numbers that is manifesting itself now.

By expanding the timescale Coughlan offered a context that went far beyond a couple of results on the playing field. The decline in playing numbers was one of the results, both direct and indirect, of decisions taken in Cork in the sixties and seventies which now bite in earnest on the northside, and not just for sports teams in that part of the city.

Situating Cork Institute of Technology/Regional Technical College, Cork University Hospital/Regional Hospital, the IDA Technology Park and the area headquarters of FÁS, the ESB and the Cork Gas Company on the southside of the city created a lopsided city in terms of economic development across many metrics, not just in state and semi-state institutions.

The week the Glen were relegated the *Examiner* ran a piece commemorating 25 years of winners of Company of the Year in Cork. The cast list included Irish Distillers, Eli Lilly, Boston Scientific, Stryker, EMC, Johnson Controls, Opera Lane, Ronan Daly Jermyn and Musgrave, none of which were located north of the river Lee.

It wasn't picking the Model Farm Road for a third-level institution fifty years ago that stopped Glen Rovers scoring enough to avoid relegation, of course. But if a GAA club reflects its community, it also reflects the reality that community faces. The thousands of jobs created by the institutions mentioned above generated the need for house-building referred to by Denis Coughlan.

Those houses in turn keep playing numbers high in clubs by feeding through occupants as participants. Or children, as they're also known. Children mean schools, of course, and that means other societal issues. For instance, the decline in vocations for the priesthood and loss of appetite for boarding school enrolment had an impact on Glen Rovers, Na Piarsaigh and other clubs on the northside: when St Finbarr's Farranferris, the diocesan semi-nary, closed, that shut off a traditional supply line of players.

Demographics pinched elsewhere, too. An ageing pop-ulation has had an impact on other schools, as Donal O'Grady sketched out some years ago:

In the forties fellas came from Innishannon to the North Mon in one direction, from Killeagh in another. Now the former would go to Hamilton HS in Bandon, the latter to Midleton CBS. Also, as community schools and so on opened around Cork in the eighties, the population in the city was ageing, so numbers in the Mon primary started to go down even as numbers from outside primary schools went on to other schools.

O'Grady's point about falling numbers in primary schools is visible in the likes of Scoil Íosagáin in Farranree. That school provided plenty of players to both Na Piarsaigh and Glen Rovers when those clubs dominated underage competitions in the seventies, both locally and nationally. Eight of the nine Féile na nGael competitions between 1973 and 1982 were won by one of those two clubs. But Scoil Íosagáin has also changed considerably since its peak enrolment of 700. Nowadays it has fewer than half that number in its classrooms, shrinking the supply line even more.

Even apparently encouraging statistics can deceive. A northside school – Christian Brothers College (CBC), a traditional rugby powerhouse – contested two of the last six Harty Cup finals. The school decided to offer hurling when, as Donal O'Mahony of CBC told the *Examiner* a couple of years ago, they noticed 'cohorts of fellas coming in from places where hurling was strong – Glounthaune, Douglas, Blackrock, Inniscarra, Blarney – and some of them weren't playing rugby'. In catering for those hurlers, he added, CBC benefited from another societal development: 'There's a change in dynamics . . . a lot of our fellas, their parents would be working in the city and it is easier to drop them to us and collect them in the evening.'

On paper, then, Cork's northside has enjoyed a healthy presence in the top tier of colleges hurling. In reality the benefit accrues more to clubs such as Erin's Own (Glounthaune), Douglas, Blackrock, Inniscarra and Blarney, none of them clubs on the northside of the city.

This leads to a pretty obvious question. Where are the people who were unable to build or buy on Cork's northside, those who might otherwise be energising clubs there?

Look at Cork's dormitory ring of suburbs and towns, which are also dominating hurling, particularly in the east: Glanmire and Riverstown (Sarsfields); Midleton; and the entire Cork–Youghal corridor, which supplies the Imokilly divisional team. In some cases an experienced eye can pick out a surname or two on teams in this area that is synonymous with a northside club, clear evidence that the son has thrown in with the local outfit rather than the parents' home club. It makes sense for a child to play with their own friends at the local club rather than travelling to line out with strangers in his parents' home place. But is Cork's northside an accommodating place for those who wish to come back and pitch in?

It's a grim joke in Glen Rovers that a dual carriageway *connects* traditional rivals Blackrock and St Finbarr's: the Rockies can jump on the South Ring Road at the Mahon exit and head west, making a right off the Ring Road onto the Togher Road and in to face the Barrs. On the northside of the river, however, a dual carriageway *divides* traditional rivals Glen Rovers and Na Piarsaigh.

For those unfamiliar with the geography, Cork City Council hung a four-lane motorway above the suburb of Blackpool, because nothing improves the quality of urban life quite like the thunder of traffic rumbling overhead 24 hours a day, a notion of city planning that has been out of date everywhere else since Robert Moses was flattening the Bronx in the fifties but which persists on the northside of Cork. The concrete curve is a grievous blow to a proud community's sense of itself, which is a potent currency for any sports club, but on a more practical level it makes accessing sports facilities on the northside of the city more difficult for all and particularly for children. The time when kids could stroll from Farranree to the Glen Field, or from Blackpool up to Na Piarsaigh, came to a halt as soon as the first eighteen-wheeler rolled along the new flyover from the Mallow Road.

For those living east of the city who might want to come back to help their clubs on the northside, the infrastructure certainly militates against it. By contrast, the route to Blackrock or St Finbarr's is a good deal smoother, thanks to the South Ring Road. And the Jack Lynch Tunnel, if you have a taste for irony.

Lynch, one of the all-time Irish sports immortals, also figures in another obstacle, though tangentially. The organisation that should be addressing the decline over years of Gaelic games on the northside of the city is the Cork County Board, and it is clearly aware of the issue. In 2016 a board officer published an ambitious plan for Gaelic games in the county which included 'The Jack Lynch Project– A Hurling Regeneration Model for Cork City'. This was intended to 'address the decline of hurling in the heartland of Cork city . . . a three-year programme for children aged 6 and 7 years in Senior Infants and First Class in all city schools and clubs . . . from late 2016 to mid 2019.' Again, extraneous matters intervened. The vast debts incurred by the redevelopment of Páirc Uí Chaoimh seem to be the focus of Cork GAA officials, rather than projects to regenerate hurling in the city. Perhaps it'll begin in 2026.

Unbalanced economic development, poor infrastructure, shrinking school enrolments, a lack of leadership – the challenges facing the northside of the city filter through to its GAA clubs and might appear to be overwhelming.

Yet Glen Rovers are also in the middle of an ambitious refurbishment project costing hundreds of thousands of euros that will update and improve their facilities significantly. The Glen's Robert Downey, a 2024 All Star along with his younger brother Eoin, was appointed Cork senior hurling captain for 2025.

And one of the largest strategic housing developments in the history of the state is planned for a part of Ballyvolane which is almost visible from the Glen Field. In time it may provide the most precious commodity for any sports club: people.

What do they get in return for membership? The dividend may be hard to quantify for outsiders, but the clubs on the northside of Cork city equip their members with resilience, self-belief and spirit, the only answer to decades of institutional neglect.

When Glen Rovers sought funding to build a club hall over seventy years ago Jack Lynch, then a young TD, was its representative in negotiations for funding. A bank manager reputedly told him that there was no collateral for the loan he was seeking. 'The people of Blackpool are my collateral,' said Lynch. He got the loan. The hall was built. In 2024 Glen Rovers defeated Blarney to return to the top tier of Cork club hurling.

WHEN THREE BECOME ONE ... EVENTUALLY

In February 2025 the GAA's Steering Group on Integration (SGI) reflected on the steady progress made on integration up to that date and looked forward to an engaging and busy year ahead for the remainder of 2025.

Apologies if that reads like a press release, but that's because it was. This was part of an update given by the SGI on its work; it had 'focused on strategic future planning to ensure significant and consistent strides are made towards Integration. There was continued collaboration with working groups to consider practical implications and actions and the commencement of projects which will ensure the implementation of integration along with ongoing engagement with Government to provide updates on the process.'

For readers still awake it's worth pointing out that some of the areas under discussion included 'Communications, Facilities, Finance, Fixtures, Games Development, HR, Membership and Match Officials, to name only a few.'

As SGI chairperson, Dr Mary McAleese noted in the statement that the project was well under way but reminded everyone of an earlier warning: 'there would be considerable work needed to align all the many moving parts, and that work has been ongoing ever since and at pace'.

Those moving parts include the Camogie Association and the Ladies' Gaelic Football Association (LGFA), of course, and aligning those isn't always straightforward at all.

When Cork won the All-Ireland senior camogie title in 2024, Camogie Association President Brian Molloy handed over the O'Duffy Cup to Cork co-captains Méabh Cahalane and Molly Lynch. In his speech Molloy said:

A hundred and twenty years ago, before the foundation of the State, our association was founded by a group of strong-willed, independent women . . . Twenty years earlier, the GAA hadn't provided for camogie, so in 1904 camogie provided for camogie. Since then, our game has developed. Our players are top level athletes who will never get boxed in.

We have more members, more clubs and more games than ever. We have a positive relationship with the GAA and are on the path to integration with them. We will integrate our organisation, we will integrate our operations, but we will retain our game, we will retain our ethos. We are camogie and we will remain camogie.

The speech wasn't welcomed by the GAA, particularly as its Central Council had provided a significant financial subvention to the Camogie Association to help with its players' charter. 'Provocative' was one senior GAA figure's description of the comments.

The annual report of the LGFA's chief executive officer Helen O'Rourke also caused waves when it came into the public domain early in 2025. O'Rourke was unambiguous about the LGFA's relationship with the GPA: 'We genuinely believe that having a positive working relationship with the GPA can be beneficial to all but believe me this can be challenging. There must be give and take on both sides and not always the expectation that change lies with the governing body, and GPA demands must always be met.' That 'believe me this can be challenging' raised eyebrows in GPA headquarters, but readers with good memories may have a better memory of O'Rourke's comments on the sport's fans:

> None of the above possible reasons take from the fact that many of our own members are the worst supporters of our game and with a membership of over 200,000 we must continue to try to change mindsets and indifferences that exist in wanting to be in attendance on one of the greatest days in our calendar year.

Criticising your own supporters is an interesting approach, but it certainly gives some added context to the 'moving parts' mentioned above.

The challenges of integration go beyond administration, of course. There are bread-and-butter issues to be addressed, and as Barry Kelly pointed out, there can be unintended consequences.

'Obviously you'd like to think it'll be a good thing, but there are very, very few female referees out there in all codes, and that is an issue in the sense that obviously, the growth of the LGFA in particular over the last twenty to twenty-five years has been phenomenal and laudable – but referees are needed for those additional games.

'Here in Westmeath if there are one or two female referees, that's as much as we have, but the traditional referees – boys and men – are being drawn to LGFA games. The game might be easier to referee, which is what I hear anecdotally: you get less grief.

'In some cases if a referee has an under-sixteen boys' match between two local clubs or an under-fifteen girls' match and he's going to get the same fee for both, then discretion is the better part of valour. If you know you're going to have much less grief at the girls' match then you'll do that one. There's an onus on the women's association to find referees rather than just depend on the existing referees who are nurtured and trained and brought up in the GAA. It's not just one challenge to the GAA in terms of integration – sharing facilities and pitches and all of that is one part of it, but refereeing is a huge challenge.'

Kelly's points are well made. Because the GAA reflects Irish society it shouldn't be assumed that the Association is a repository of enlightenment at all times. I recall having a cuppa with a senior administrator in a prominent county who prefaced some remarks so old-fashioned they were antediluvian with an honest assessment of his own position: 'I suppose I'm a bit of an oul' chauvinist.'

By the same token, however, attitudes are changing. Anthony O'Connor of the Ballinteer St John's club in south Dublin offered some compelling evidence.

'The girls are very sensitive to equality, which is a good thing. But something that's really impressed me about the young men in our club is we've had a couple of issues over the years where the men's footballers and the women's camogie team have wanted the same pitch at the same time, and it's caused big problems.

'There was one issue where there was a clash about a pitch. Men's football wanted it and sort of pulled rank to get their own way, but the girls actually went to the lads and said, "This is bullshit. We've had that pitch booked and we want it". And in fairness the lads took that on board and went to their own mentors to say, "You're not acting for us here." I was terribly impressed by that – really, really good young people.'

Wearing his medical hat – he is head of gastroenterology at Tallaght University Hospital and clinical professor in gastroenterology at TCD – O'Connor pointed to specific challenges for female athletes.

'We've a base of about a hundred adult women players, and over the course of the last eighteen months, eight of them have had anterior cruciate ligament injuries. So that's eight per cent of our adult female playing populations. Women are far more likely to do their ACLs than men and there are various reasons for that, some of which are related to hormones and the time of the woman's cycle. Interestingly, girls who are under the contraceptive pill are significantly less likely to pick up that injury because of a hormone that the female body produces called relaxin. What that's for is childbirth, basically to allow the bones of the pelvis to separate a little. And that gets released at certain times in the cycle and when that's highest in the blood is when a woman is most susceptible to [ACL injury]. So that's something you can't really change.

'Another thing is that a lot of clubs now will be putting boys on strength and conditioning programmes in the mid-teens, and now that's happening with girls. In the club we've worked on that, though not as "strength and conditioning", we don't like that term. We preferred to focus on athletic development in terms of landing mechanics and quads-to-hamstrings ratios and things like that – that's where you can really make a difference.

'I've written a paper, a proposal for our club that we would invest in a screening programme for good players starting off; we pilot up with them and then maybe roll it out across a bigger group, where we actually look at people's landing mechanics, look at their quads–hamstring–glutes ratios, and see who's most at risk of an ACL injury and then come up with interventions and implement interventions for that.

'Women are more likely to do their cruciate and more likely to redo their cruciate. And women are far more likely than men to give up sports after a cruciate – about thirty per cent more likely – so that's a big issue.'

All of which exists in the shadow of a classic male–female sports error; using the model for male development with women as well, which is the kind of mistake feminist advocate Caroline Criado-Perez identifies in her work, but there may be specific GAA-type issues to consider here.

O'Connor says:

'I'm not a massive fan of the development squad model. I think in Dublin . . . you had a very successful development squad programme on the men's side and . . . they tried to implement the same thing with girls, but it's not the same.

'Coaching girls is not the same as coaching boys. Sometimes it can be hard to find words around this without sounding misogynistic, but the girls have to be happy. You can have tension in the group of lads, and sometimes it can push them on. But the girls, they have to be happy to come to training. They tend to have a broader range of interests than the lads as well. We have one girl who's a fantastic corner back, but really her passion is acting.

'It's not just sport a lot of the time, either. The lads may be trying to combine rugby or soccer or something with hurling and football, but the girls will quite often be interested in something outside sport. We have one girl who was a Dublin under-sixteen camogie player, a phenomenal athlete, but she's a concert pianist as well. Different interests.

'I have twins, one boy and one girl, and I used to do both their groups when they were under eight, under nine, stuff like that. And if you had sixty boys down to the training session, we as the coaches could throw in a couple of footballs, and even if you went across to the clubhouse for a couple of pints and came back an hour later, they'd still be playing football. The girls, if you did something like that and went off, when you came back four or five would be playing football. Four or five would [be playing] duck-duck-goose, four or five would be doing cartwheels and so on. The sessions work a little bit differently.

'There's also huge benefits in terms of your coaching, because the girls will challenge you a little bit more. "What's this going to do? Why are we doing this now? How is this going to improve us?" They're more mature in that way.

'What I always said when I was chair of our club, ninety per cent of the problems in the club had nothing to do with players or games. Of the small percentage that came from players and games, ninety per cent of those came with underage female teams. And of course, ninety per cent of the problems had nothing to do with the girls themselves but usually fathers – sometimes mothers but often fathers. Sometimes that was rugby dads taking over teams and setting things up a certain way. Sometimes it was the child getting into a development squad with Dublin, and then she knew everything and the club knew nothing. But when she got spat out down the line by the development squad system she was just back with the club.

'People think amalgamation is going to just be, "Well, everything we do for the boys, we're now going to do it for the girls as well." That's not going to fly. There are extra things that the girls will need. Injury prevention is huge, and I think if the GAA were looking for quick wins to set up integration, funding academic research into why girls get cruciate injuries, for instance, would be huge because that would roll on into screening programmes across the sport. Our finest player in our club is Laura Nolan, won a couple of All-Irelands with Dublin, and she was one of the cruciate victims. Just phenomenal, a great human being, really. And when she did her cruciate there was a pall over the whole club for a couple of weeks afterwards. I'd been banging the drum for ages on cruciate injuries so I've been commissioned by our club to write a report into it, and we will be looking for a screening programme and hopefully get funded. Or we can fundraise around it, you know. That whole aspect of the thing is a big challenge for integration.'

A challenge, but also an opportunity? O'Connor's point about cruciate research being an easy win is a good one. Are there others? Camogie and ladies' football may not be doing themselves too many favours with public pronouncements, but could the GAA be more proactive?

The point could be made that the GAA, with its position of dominance, could take the high road and embrace integration enthusiastically, stressing the power of shared facilities as investment in a common future rather than a short-term cost. A small change in terminology, perhaps, but if we learn anything in this book we'll learn how significant small changes in rhetoric can be.

Publicity missteps notwithstanding, the two women's organisations have done a terrific job from a low base of finance and resources: the two sports are manifestly better now than they were and are more widely played, a clear endorsement of the work of those organisations. Observers have also pointed out that many clubs are far ahead of the governing bodies in terms of local arrangements with all sports – the One Club model offers a framework for that co-operation – but the importance of top-level administrators can't be overlooked either. With their resources, and the stability of staff in key positions which helps with building the relationships necessary to drive integration, they should be able to drive agreement on this.

The focus on women's sport now is laudable but there's also a chance to broaden the focus. The GAA has worked on wheelchair hurling, for instance; are there other opportunities to get under-represented groups involved in Gaelic games?

The community ethos of the GAA should be well suited to more initiatives like wheelchair hurling if the desire is there. The desire to see an investment instead of a cost, and to see the opportunity rather than the crisis.

PART 2
REVENUE

BOTTOM LINES AND GOOD TIMING

When it comes to the GAA's contribution to Irish society the rhetoric can trump the detail pretty quickly, and as will become obvious elsewhere in this book, GAA rhetoric often needs a considerable amount of focus and tightening to begin with.

The usual bullet points are community spirit and a volunteer ethos, with a general nod towards the value of a GAA club in its parish or suburb. Long on the intangibles, light on the figures. I brought up this subject a couple of times when I was writing *GAAconomics* some years ago, but even GAA figures threw up their hands: how could you put an exact figure on what the GAA was contributing everywhere and at every level in the country?

Credit to the GAA, then, for coming up with a way to put a precise number on that figure. In late November 2024 the Association issued a press statement giving a breakdown of a report it had commissioned on its value and return on investment, which it claimed was the first of its kind in Irish sport. The analysis was carried out by Sheffield Hallam University, and according to the GAA's statement:

This independent analysis of Gaelic games activity by international experts has found that the Social Value of Gaelic games is estimated to be worth at least €2.87 billion to Irish society.

The Social Return on Investment study shows that for every one euro invested in Gaelic games, the benefit returned to society is at least €2.30 and could be as much as €3.96.

The GAA, LGFA and Camogie Association commissioned Sheffield Hallam University's Sport Industry Research Group, who are pioneers in the economics of sport and sport's wider social impacts. Assisted by colleagues in Manchester Metropolitan University and Ulster University, they have spent the last 13 months working on this project.

It is based, in part, on the analysis of national, provincial, county and more than 500 club accounts from across Gaelic games and establishes for the first time the economic impact of Gaelic games activity across the 32 counties and the Social Value of the work of more 1,600 clubs which are led by volunteers. It is also the first time in Irish sport that a report of this detail has looked at the totality of impact from economic to social value to specific major events.

Analysis of the social value of Gaelic games activity estimates that an input or spend to produce Gaelic games of €1.244 billion, resulted in outcomes valued to Irish life worth €2.87 billion.

- €31.06 million for Health,
- €556.48 million for Subjective Wellbeing,
- €1.224 billion for Social Capital, and
- €1.056 billion for the replacement cost of volunteering.

Detailed event impact assessment of major provincial finals shows that the 2024 Ulster Senior Football Championship Final was worth €1.5 million to the town of Clones and in total €2.1 million to County Monaghan. The

2024 Munster Senior Hurling Championship Final was worth €3.2 million to the town of Thurles and €4.5 million to County Tipperary.

A Satellite Account for Sport extracts its values from the System of National Accounts. The Satellite Account for Gaelic games reveals that:

- Consumer spending on Gaelic games is €377m, which equates to 7.8% of the sport industry;
- Gross Value Added attributable to Gaelic games is €710 million (8.7% of the sport industry);
- Employment generated by Gaelic games is 10,600 FTE (9.8% of the sport industry);
- Total economic activity attributable to Gaelic games is €1,619 million (10.2% of the sport industry); Government receives €192.6 million in direct and indirect taxation from Gaelic games.

Lead researcher Professor Simon Shibli said: 'This report shows that Gaelic games is good for the economy and good for society.'

Uachtarán CLG Jarlath Burns said: 'For the first time the Association has been able to secure facts and figures that confirm what we have always known – that Gaelic games activity makes an enormously positive impact on society through our involvement in communities, and that this in turn, benefits the economy all across the island.'

The president went on to show that the report proved how large a contribution the GAA makes and has made to Irish society and he thanked Professor Shibli and his team for their work.

Apologies for the lengthy quotation, but it's worth having the facts and figures close at hand. Particularly given what happened not long afterwards.

The Sheffield report was published on 27 November and in early December John Fogarty of the *Irish Examiner* dropped a bombshell: the Revenue Commissioners were taking a very close look at the accounts of several counties. They had not accepted a €119,778 voluntary disclosure Mayo made pertaining to legacy issues around payments to Cúl Camp coaches in 2018 and 2019, and Mayo had had to postpone its annual convention because of that issue. Galway officers did not confirm their accounts pending a risk review of 2018 and 2019, while for the same period Wexford made a voluntary disclosure of €55,000 to Revenue under the heading of team administration.

When the news broke a chill gripped treasurers all over the country, and the nervousness was compounded by remarks made at the Wexford county convention by the outgoing county chairman, Micheál Martin. He told delegates at the convention that if there was to be consistency, the likelihood was that all counties, potentially clubs too, and other sporting bodies would all be subjected to Revenue inspection for matters such as payments to referees.

An appalling vista appeared.

The GAA's annual congress early in 2025 already had plenty to discuss. The new football rules, the ongoing back-and-forth about a possible Katie Taylor fight, the prospect of a first National Football League (NFL) game in Croke Park, the usual discussion of income: a full raft of topics were on the agenda for the get-together in Donegal. However, one contribution helped to lower the blood pressure of treasurers all over the country, and not just those operating at county level. At the congress the GAA's national finance committee chairman Feargal

McCormack outlined the details of the process by which the 26 GAA county boards in the jurisdiction of the Republic of Ireland would be subject to self-risk reviews after discussions between Croke Park and the Revenue Commissioners.

McCormack told delegates that the GAA leadership had contacted Revenue in December to 'manage and mitigate the stress' of risk reviews on volunteers and officers, adding that the mechanisms of the mass disclosures were currently being finalised with Revenue, though he provided details on the way forward. Counties would make a self-declaration for an agreed four-year period (2021–2024), based on their calculation for 2024, which would 'hopefully allow officers to reference their most recent findings and records . . . The findings in this year will then be extrapolated out to determine any liability for the years 2021 to 2023.' The liabilities would be divided into six core payments – managers, backroom team members, players, full-time county staff, casual staff and volunteers, and referees (though it was believed that there would be no tax liabilities relating to referees). McCormack went on to assure those in attendance that the self-assessment would be 'significantly less demanding than a full Revenue audit'. Good news for treasurers everywhere, particularly after the uncomfortable headlines of a few weeks previously.

In retrospect, the panic about the Revenue news – the concern that those investigations would spill over into every unit of the GAA – looks a little overblown. At the time it was pointed out that such investigations had the potential to capsize voluntary organisations all over Ireland. Who would be willing to lend an hour or two to help with the administration of their local Tidy Towns committee or church choir, let alone their local GAA club, if they might end up picking their way through onerous financial compliance procedures in an airless meeting room with the Revenue Commissioners?

There was quite a lot of talk then about the social capital generated by the GAA and other organisations, about the possibility people would abandon such small-scale community organisations and about the damage done to the social fabric of the country in that kind of scenario. It soon emerged that Revenue was more interested in bigger units of the GAA, hence the soothing words at Congress about counties facing interactions with the state body that would be significantly less demanding than full audits.

Yet there's another way of looking at the Revenue investigations. As outlined by a member of the GAA's own 2034 Committee, the Revenue Commissioners could be the saviours of amateurism in the GAA, particularly if they focused on one of the biggest problems in the Association. Ger Aherne of the 2034 Committee was blunt in his assessment of amateurism and paid managers in the GAA when he spoke to John Fogarty of the *Examiner* early in 2025:

> If you go through the books of county boards and clubs, they will say that person A was remunerated last month for X number of kilometres at the public service rate and reimbursed for expenses, but is that the totality of the remuneration for people managing and coaching in the GAA? We adequately covered these issues in our report, that the professional services that are used by counties and clubs such as physiotherapists and accountants have to be remunerated. It is the coaching, managing and playing that is the issue for the GAA's amateur status.
>
> The truth is that one of the saviours of the GAA and amateurism might be the Revenue Commissioners. You have to understand that a lot of these illegal payments are off balance sheets. If some of these travelling mercenary

managers at club and county level were subject to Revenue audits, it would be interesting. The recommendation was to bring legitimate allowances for managers and players into the foreground and not the background. I'm not so sure the allowances in the foreground now cover the totality of the payments being made and that's where the Revenue Commissioners might come in.

We're either interested in saving the organisation or we're not. I'm increasingly hearing from the generation after me about how sick and tired they are and how lukewarm they are about the organisation because of the GAA saying one thing and not doing what is required to bring that about.

You see a lot of clubs having a competition for who their manager is going to be. Rather than going down the multi-annual process of preparing their own people for management and coaching, they want to go for the quick hit. 'Let's pay €20,000 or €30,000 to Johnny Go Backwards who is a, b and c.' That's where club committees are contributing to all of this. If the recommendation that only club members can manage their clubs was accepted, people would say, 'Anyone can be a member of a club,' but that's not true. This is all about the willingness or lack of willingness to actually police ourselves.

Aherne's focus on payments to managers is spot on. But before we talk mercenaries, as he says, and not missionaries, we need to acknowledge something. Preparing inter-county teams costs money. A lot of money.

AND NOT FORGETTING THAT MASSIVE BAG OF JAFFA CAKES

Everyone has an abstract idea of the costs involved in preparing elite GAA teams, but concrete details can still give you pause. That was certainly the case in early 2025, when the GAA revealed that the collective profits of county boards had fallen in 2024 and were down to €1.8 million from €4.1 million in 2023.

Why? The fall was put down to the spend on inter-county team preparation, and that spend, for 2024, came to €44 million. GAA director general Tom Ryan said at the time that it was the responsibility of individual counties as well as the GAA centrally to help rein in that spending, adding that it needed to be tackled:

> It's difficult to see how the level we have now, where that's going to take us in five to ten years' time if we don't arrest it. So, what it means is: Spending less, expending less effort, a collective acknowledgement on the part of everybody that we centralise procurement and put some of the burden on this table here [Central Council], whether that be travel or related ancillary services. It just means thinking about things differently.
>
> If I knew how we were going to solve it, it would have been solved by now. There's an awful lot that's really, really good about the inter-county season. We need to be careful that we don't damage it when we undertake that. But we're at the stage now where if we're still having the same conversation in five or ten years, it'll be too late, really.

This can't continue. We're in an arms race. How can this be sustained? And where will it all end?

What isn't asked quite as often is a more specific question. Where does that money go? How is so much being spent? In fact, quite a few of the club delegates who get sent along to those conventions where county secretaries intone staggering figures often ponder that question: how are we spending that much money?

Welcome, then, to a training session for the senior team from an unnamed but representative county, where we'll carry out an analysis. Not of the sprints or the shooting but the spending.

In your mind's eye imagine the team in mid-drill at a training session and freeze the picture: a dozen players are here in a small-sided game, a dozen over here working out a couple of defensive scenarios, free-takers over there, the keepers being tested in goal with a few close-in shots. In terms of cost, we'll be conservative, but it all adds up.

We'll start at the end of the session: every person frozen in mid-stride gets a full meal after training, which means 35 meals multiplied by €10: €350. But wait: there are at least a dozen members of the backroom team also on hand: add another €120. Eight of the players are students in third-level institutions who are not in their home county: the round trip is a hundred miles to training at standard GAA expense rates, 50c a mile. Eight x €50: €400. At least ten of the other players also travel a hundred miles for training. Ten x €50: €500.

Two of the players can be glimpsed in the top corner of your mental picture. They're not training. They picked up pretty serious injuries at the very start of the season and are out of action for several months. However, because they were injured on county duty the county board pays a discretionary amount to each to make up the shortfall in their wages: it's a weekly amount but for our purposes it equates to two players getting €150 each per session: €300.

Professional expertise is on hand for the panel. There are two masseurs and physios in attendance, right next to those two injured players. They are paid €100 each: €200. The strength and conditioning coach is in the centre of the field and keeping an eye on the players' physical progression: he's getting €100 for the session. There are two individuals with laptops at the halfway line; they're performance analysts who are logging data for a debrief later with the management team. They're getting €150 each per session: €300.

Then there's the equipment. That adds up fast. Those bulging sacks at each corner of the field? They all contain fruit and snacks – oranges, Jaffa Cakes, energy drinks and so forth – which are usually kept in the dressing room but are on the field tonight for ease of access to the players: €200. The team's training gear is personalised and paid for by the county board and is freshly laundered every week: €50. (This team is a football side, by the way, which doesn't incur one of the great GAA expenses: new sliotars, which is a cost of at least €100 per night.)

We're not done yet. County teams have a logistics man who usually drives a van with the team equipment. The van is sponsored, usually, but there are running costs, such as maintenance, insurance and diesel, which we'll round off to €30 per session. Also, while some counties have their own training grounds, many have to rent pitches from clubs and schools in the county: say €100 per session. And even if the county has its own centre of excellence, there is the cost of maintenance, floodlights at certain times of the year, water, rates, insurance . . . Let's round it up to €100.

All in? A session leaves you with little change out of €2,600, and that's for training pure and simple. It doesn't count the cost of transport, food and accommodation if the team has an overnight stay for a league or championship game, for instance. Nor does it begin to cover warm-weather training in Spain or Portugal or even a camp in a hotel resort in Ireland.

But it gives you a hint of the expense: three sessions a week from January to July – and many counties make it to July or very close to that nowadays – means 12 sessions a month, 84 sessions in total, and a bill of €218,400.

If you're from the west coast, don't lose your voice shouting: obviously players from counties along the Atlantic travel further and have more players coming back from Dublin and other cities.

In addition, for our purposes the injury costs are consciously kept down in our example. Readers will be well aware of inter-county managers pointing to injury lists of a dozen players or more at various times in the season.

These are the sorts of figures which result in the GAA declaring, as it did in 2025, that elite team preparation costs over €40 million, an eye-watering sum.

But what about the figures that aren't as freely available? What about the sums paid under the table and off the books, a phenomenon described in the past as a cancer within the GAA?

THE BIGGEST THREAT TO THE FUTURE OF THE GAA

This is how the conversation goes.

Johnny Green is at home watching the TV when his phone rings. It's an unknown number, but that's not unusual: as a former inter-county star working in sales he's used to random callers looking to talk about the products he's selling as well as the most recent games. And he keeps a separate phone for family members in any case. He's also used to random callers making contact for a very specific reason. In any event, he answers.

'Is this Johnny? Paddy Brown here, how are you doing?'

There's some chit-chat first: only to be expected. Johnny's years of meeting people after matches all over the country have given him a line of bland generalities he can trot out with little effort until Paddy gets to the point, which he eventually does.

'Look, Johnny, I'm involved with the Rovers here, as you might be aware.'

By saying he's 'involved' rather than chairman or secretary Paddy is making a subtle point. He's indicating that while he is empowered to speak on that club's behalf, there is also a level of deniability when it comes to the next phase of the conversation. That may prove important at a future club AGM, but for the moment that doesn't detain the two lads, because by introducing this subtle acknowledgement into the chat, Paddy is building to the purpose of his call . . .

'We're looking around for a coach. A good one. We're going well but we want to drive it on. Anyway, we were thinking of

Billy White and I know you know him well, sure the two of ye played together long enough.'

Now we're getting to it.

Johnny talks about his old teammate Billy for a bit. Yes, he's a good coach, and yes, he's available. In fact, it just so happens that Johnny and Billy are meeting up for a game of golf at the weekend. Paddy knows their golf plans well, of course, having done his due diligence, but Johnny isn't going to upset the decorum of the call by acknowledging that. There are specific roles to play here, after all.

'Look,' says Johnny after a minute or two of singing his golf partner's praises when planning training drills and making crucial in-game switches, 'he's going to want to know what's involved, obviously.'

Paddy knows what this means as soon as it's said and comes out with it straight: 'Eighteen. Use of a car.'

'Hm,' says Johnny, looking out of his window at the car sitting in his own driveway. The licence plate shows the car was registered a whole eight years ago. Then he waits.

'Of course', says Paddy, 'if you were interested yourself it would be more.'

'Let me think about it,' says Johnny. 'I have your number here anyway.'

Paddy says no problem, and when he hangs up he texts the club chairman who deputed him to make the call, telling him the man they want is interested alright; and by the end of the week Rovers have their new coach.

Johnny, of course.

The discussion about Johnny's old teammate and his undoubted coaching ability – even if his availability for the job in question was never absolutely and categorically confirmed – was just a formality. The kind of courtship ritual David

Attenborough usually describes in an excited whisper when recording his voiceovers. Billy was just one of the possible coaches used as an opening gambit by a club intent on landing a bigger fish. That's an understood part of the pantomime.

Johnny won't be sharing the details of that conversation with anyone, least of all Billy. Nor will Paddy, come to that. Neither would be interested in drawing too much attention to the ritual, and in fact both may suffer from a sort of localised amnesia if they're ever quizzed on timelines and details of the appointment. 'Approaches' is about as specific as anyone is likely to get.

Don't feel too sorry for Billy, though. If he was in serious contention for the job of coaching the Rovers he'll figure in another conversation sooner or later. Someone will ask loaded questions about a coach of his acquaintance, and then the chat will turn, and a few months later he'll be able to upgrade his car. Just like Johnny.

Welcome to the strange world of the paid GAA manager, where cash incentives, perks such as apartment use and car models are the grammar of interaction. 'Twilight' was my first impulse when it came to describing this world, but it hardly does justice to this mysterious economy, which exists in the shadows, away from yet parallel with real life. This parallel economy will, if nothing else, plunge you into some very unusual conversations.

For instance, you may find yourself discussing a small rural club that is somehow – somehow! – paying a coach almost €30,000 to take on its sole adult team and justifying the expenditure on the basis that this coach is bringing in a strength and conditioning trainer as well. Which therefore means two management figures for the price of one. Kind of.

Or you may end up chatting to a friend of yours from a club that is looking for a specific individual who is well known for his coaching prowess. Said individual may have quoted a figure of over €300 a night to train your mate's club, but there is a significant proviso. The club will have to organise training for Tuesdays and Thursdays, because the individual concerned is already committed to a club in a different county on Monday and Wednesday evenings. In order for him to pocket €1,200 in cash every week the two clubs' training sessions can't clash.

Or you may end up talking idly to a club officer about his club's management team, a conversation in which you wonder what a particular person you glimpsed on the sideline at a match is contributing to the club. The response may be a terse one, with the officer saying – through gritted teeth – that the players wanted this person along as a sports psychologist, that the officer has yet to see him at a training session, that his contribution in the dressing room before games appears limited to roaring 'Focus!' at random intervals . . . but, the officer adds, the individual concerned gets an envelope with cash every Friday evening at the clubhouse. As does the actual manager of the club team, who is a relative of the 'sports psychologist'.

All of these scenarios may be true, but there's a catch-22 of sorts at work. It's impossible to report on these matters in the media for the simple reason that they're practically impossible to prove. It's accepted that clubs all over Ireland are paying managers, but standing that up in a court of law would defeat Woodward and Bernstein. At least they had a paper trail that could be followed, while GAA club management must be the last remaining commercial space in western Europe where cash is still king.

By the same token, it's possible to speculate as wildly as one likes about payment amounts. How can any of these coaches correct the record? 'How dare you say I got forty thousand euro from that club when I only got thirty thousand' is not a defence one hears, for fairly obvious reasons to do with the Revenue Commissioners' lack of humour about undisclosed earnings.

Lest there be any misconceptions, paid managers are a cancer in the GAA. That's what Christy Cooney said when he was president of the Association, and he was absolutely correct. The paid manager runs contrary to the ethos of the GAA in both the letter and spirit of the law. It undercuts the meaning of a club and also points out that club's shortcomings if it cannot produce a manager from its own ranks.

Taking a wider view, the paid manager is a hypocrite whose exploitation of a club, or a county, is a fundamental contradiction of the GAA's commitment to community and voluntarism: it is both bare-faced extortion and shameless exploitation, and the paid manager's tenure always taints the ecosystem he leaves behind. This betrayal of the GAA's core principles has now been accepted to the point that media coverage routinely cites extensions and contracts and deals when writing about managers, terms more appropriate to professional sport. In what other sphere of Irish life would so many people not only break the law in full view but do so under the hot glare of publicity?

All over Ireland, when the mercenary has moved onto his next stop on the circuit and the club holds its AGM, some version of this statement can be heard when the top table seeks nominations from the floor for manager of the club's top team.

'Chairman,' someone will say, 'with all due respect, how do you expect one of us to do for nothing what you paid the last man thousands of euro to do?'

Almost inevitably, it was Dara Ó Cinnéide who crystallised the conversation about paid managers:

'Recently enough I was chatting to a few lads in the club and we were discussing a management team for the seniors.

One of the lads said, "Would you not just go outside the club?" And I said we could quite easily, but it would break my heart because if we did I'd have to cut all ties with the club after all those years. I'd walk away because I'd be betraying everything I believe.

'In fairness, the chap who asked then said, "Fair enough, I get it." My point to him was that we could quite easily get a very good coach or manager – someone who might very well win a title with the team – but I also felt I'd have to live with that decision for the rest of my life. And I didn't want to reach a point where I didn't believe in the club: I admitted to him I could get emotional about it, but that there were certain principles worth holding.'

It was interesting that no contributor to this book disagreed about the existence of the paid club manager. Indeed, for almost all it was a given, an accepted fact of life in the GAA. Yet how can there be a situation where the manager in the dressing room is being paid while the people playing for him are not?

In October 2024 GAA President Jarlath Burns made some comments which became the newest set text on this issue when he was quoted in the *Examiner*.

> What does it mean to be a GAA inter-county player in 2024 and what does it mean to be a manager? I think there will be a debate on whether we should put managers on contract, because it is nearly a full-time job, the amount of accountability is there. Even when you are winning there can be difficulty listening to criticism.

'It's a huge issue,' said Professor Jack Anderson, specialist in sports law at the University of Melbourne (and one-time secretary of the GAA's Disputes Resolution Authority).

'Managers are being paid at inter-county level, that's just being straightforward. They are. I think Jarlath's comments were focused on the inter-county side and they're an acknowledgment of that reality, but the obvious retort is what you've said. How can it just be the manager who's being paid?

'There are all sorts of additional twists to this, too. I remember starting out in the eighties and at club AGMs lads would be saying, "We need an outside manager to come in" and all of that, but back then it was generally a manager or a coach coming in on his own. He'd probably get two selectors from the club and drive on.

'Now it's different, because even at club level a manager comes in with a coach, a strength and conditioning guy, while at inter-county level you see the size of the backroom teams. At all levels you hear that emphasised: it's not the manager, it's the team with him, the "management package", however you want to phrase that.

'Where you may end up is with a budget for inter-county teams, and managers may have to work within that budget and declare every bit of it accordingly. We've seen that in Australia with semi-professional teams in the AFL [Australian Football League]. With the GAA you may see a cap introduced, with ways around it, say if a manager or one of the selectors is a games development officer within the county as well then that could be taken into consideration with the cap. I think we could go in that direction.

'The issue then, of course, is how you cap spending, and what happens if a county breaches that cap? Will the GAA have the balls to go and punish that county properly and show there are consequences? That's done in other sports, but to enforce the cap an organisation may need an internal service checking these things and auditing spending. Would that be better than what we have now? What's there at present is certainly a sham amateurism, and sunlight is the best disinfectant.'

Irial Mac Murchú in An Rinn, west Waterford, pointed out contradictions in the outside manager cycle:

'It favours the bigger, stronger clubs which can afford to pay managers to come in, though that may seem counterintuitive because the bigger, stronger clubs have more access to in-club talent to train and develop teams. It hasn't yet hit its ceiling, I think. Our own club paid people at times over the years, but we haven't had an outside trainer for many years. Thankfully, we're strong enough to have a good selection internally ourselves. It's one of these unique GAA things, these payments under the table. [Former GAA president] Peter Quinn couldn't even find the table and I think that's a more difficult one to crack than the official spending figures.'

As the man with the legal expertise, Anderson raises a strong point about the GAA enforcing compliance with spending caps. In other leagues and sports clubs will spend money and time fighting sanctions for breaching rules like that, but there are no guarantees the GAA will enforce its own rules on this matter. Elsewhere in this book we discuss the habitual challenging of suspensions for playing offences; what chance a county board would simply accept expulsion from a provincial championship? Highly unlikely, going on past examples and the general view of the rulebook as a rough guide to negotiation.

Then there are other considerations, which could benefit the legal profession. Anderson said:

'I think that may be where Jarlath is going with payment to managers. But then that opens up a whole other vista, because once you start paying people you are obviously getting into employment law and employment rights and all that that entails. Say a paid manager's team has a bad run in the national league, and the players are getting unhappy with him, and the supporters are dissatisfied and the county board is worried . . . if the manager walks away that's fine, but what if he doesn't? If the county board wants to get rid of him then they'll have to officially terminate his employment, and that could be very messy. Or it might have to pay him off. You could end up in the Workplace Relations Commission, and that's not even taking into account the other people who may be part of his "management package". You'll see a Premier League team sack its manager and that means all the coaches and other staff are gone as well with him – all of them paid off. That's okay for a Premier League club but for a county board which may be barely keeping its head above water financially that's a daunting prospect.'

Back to the Revenue Commissioners. Is their introduction the only way to break this up?

'It's such a strange situation because essentially if the manager is being paid under the table then it's a matter of his own personal responsibility. And you don't want the tax authorities to be regulating your sport, either. In fairness that's where Jarlath is coming from. This situation is occurring in inter-county circles as it stands, so let's have a declaratory system in place.

'And of course this is happening at club level as well, which is its own separate challenge. Everyone who's involved in a club knows the lads who are out selling lotto tickets and raising funds, so there's money sloshing around a lot of clubs. Will the same system have to apply at that level? That's a reality because there are club managers being paid as well. It's one of the key strengths of any voluntary organisations that when you're working on its behalf, you're looking around at the others who are working on its behalf as well – you're not a lone soldier because everyone is volunteering together. But once that is broken, it's broken.'

As with all contributors on the topic, Anderson acknowledged the seriousness of inter-county competition for context:

'The level of commitment now at inter-county is unbelievable. It is semi-professional, or professional in all but name, and the other question is how that can be sustained. Once you reach very high standards then you can't go back – there's no going back to training Tuesdays and Thursdays for a month before the championship.

'A budget and cap at inter-county level is an obvious place to start in terms of addressing funding.'

The true strangeness of this phenomenon has barely been explored, largely because of the participants' extraordinary ability to keep their traps shut. It's very difficult to find published testimony that includes even incidental references to the paid manager, which is why credit must go to former Mayo midfielder David Brady for his honesty. Some years ago Brady told the 42 website about his experience with GAA clubs when he was looking at getting involved in management.

'But the conversations I've had, sometimes the first question is, "What is your fee? What do you expect?" At club level. I said, "Jeez, that's the first question you ask me!" And I'm going, "Jesus Christ almighty, what about 'Tell me about your ethos, tell me about your structures.'" And I know in the back of my mind in the conversation he's thinking, "How much is this guy going to cost? He's talking a serious game." And I'm going, "That's what it is."'

When Brady said such exchanges occur every 'single day of the week' he also pointed to the most obvious contradiction involved in paying a club manager: 'They are getting something because that's the expected [thing] now, that you don't do things for nothing, but the players are still expected to do it for nothing.'

A good point, and one worth teasing out further.

* * *

Discussing the paid manager phenomenon with Tom Parsons of the GPA was fruitful, because he didn't waste time on platitudes but drilled into the why and how of the problem.

'This is an issue. Why is it happening? Because there's a value set on managers. How do you set a value? By creating a transfer market. At the club level Johnny goes to the local club and says he'll train them if they cover his expenses. Then the next club over says they'll cover his expenses and add in a hot meal after training, and it all spirals from there. The transfer market causes this because you'll see what people perceive as at the true value of managers.'

Parsons floated an obvious step forward for the cohort of itinerant coaches and managers roaming Ireland:

'Is managers and coaches travelling the country like this a bad thing? In one way it is, because it might be the root cause of these problems. In another way, would we have hurling in Antrim if we didn't have this? Do we need coaches to go to lower-tier counties to raise standards? That's a positive.

'People might give out about the GPA collectively bargaining for its players. But if it weren't there, local groups of players would bargain their own rates, only to learn that other counties were getting better rates and so on.

'Maybe if managers had their own representative body to bargain collectively, something that would recognise costs and times, we wouldn't be in this position.

'There are people in the GAA who'd say the GPA is a bad thing, but I don't think we have a chance of protecting amateurism if we don't have them engaged in collective bargaining to ensure the players' deal is fair. We bargain funds for expenses, funds and scholarships, and it's the same for everyone no matter what county they play for. And that bugs some people in the GAA, but it has protected amateurism because you can't have it both ways. It's either capitalism or socialism.'

It was interesting to tease this issue out with Parsons because of the philosophical implications: if players in every county get the same rates, that's equitable, but is it fair if different counties generate different amounts of revenue? That sounds like a mix of socialism and capitalism, in one sense. And where do club players fit in?

'At a club level the county players going back there are equal with the club players. They often have to pay for socks and shorts or put petrol in the car to go to a match. Absolutely equal, as that's the tier they're playing at. But at the next tier, inter-county, the costs are the same no matter what county you're in. I think it's interesting that the costs of the inter-county game, the famous forty-four million, the players' share of that is not remuneration as much as recovering expenses, and that's seven million. Combined, the costs of management teams far exceed that. A body that would have argued for that group – managers – on rates and so on would have been beneficial twenty years ago.'

The obvious issue here, though, is that coaches and managers are sole traders by definition. Though some may work with a couple of trusted lieutenants, only one person gets the bib with BAINISTEOIR on it. They're also in direct conflict with other managers all the time. Players are in open competition with each other on the field on a Sunday, but even rivals from differ-ent counties might be working together for the same organisation in the working week. By contrast, managers have the elbows out with others as they try to get appointed to run county teams: there isn't an unlimited number of jobs, and the compe-tition is keen. That's not an environment in which one could build the trust and unity that achieves common goals, like the players' body.

The other consideration that isn't always discussed in too much detail is the enormity of the undertaking. Managing an inter-county team is an onerous undertaking, to put it mildly. The time commitment is huge. An inter-county selector once told me that the manager owned his time when he clocked out of work at half three on weekdays, and all weekend: all of his time. The selector wasn't complaining – he accepted that as part of the deal – but he pointed out that the manager was the one co-ordinating all the other members of the backroom staff. The manager must also maintain a high level of energy and positivity for the entire group at all times, ensure the logistics are first-class – players have threatened strikes over the quality of food served after training – as well as liaising with county board officials, the media and sponsors, not to mention acting in loco parentis for players who may sometimes be simultaneously extravagantly gifted athletes and immature youngsters. All of this without considering the challenge of gauging and reacting to high-pressure games in front of thousands of people.

Clearly the range of skills needed is wide, which brings us to a comment delivered with some force by a county board official on the subject of managers: the ones you can get are the ones you don't want, and the ones you want are the ones you can't get because they have better things to do. This is a phenomenon rarely discussed openly but often acknowledged privately. The people with the skills, personality and energy for inter-county management often have all those strengths recognised at work, where they are rewarded commensurately.

The sociological and historical changes that have led to this situation are not a matter for this book, but it is worth considering whether past generations of GAA members, lacking the employment opportunities of twenty-first-century Ireland, poured that extra energy and drive into their clubs and counties. One for another book, perhaps.

The end result is that the inter-county manager can raise some valid questions before he ever takes a session, as Tom Parsons points out.

'When you speak to coaches and managers at that level they say, "Hold on, for me to do this I'm going to have to go to three days a week in work, or hire a manager for my business. It's an unreasonable amount of time and commitment to give without some level of compensation, so you have to help me out. If I lose – or don't succeed, whatever that means – my professional reputation, my personal reputation will be on the line, the public will be down on top of me and I'll be sacked."'

That can lead to controversy in its own right, of course. Kerry manager Jack O'Connor hit the headlines when he admitted in his autobiography that he worked half days as a teacher in 2006 and became a full-time football manager in the afternoons, saying he was reimbursed by the Kerry County Board. 'I said to the County Board that for me this was the only way to operate. It was done,' he wrote. The Kerry County Board denied that the arrangement existed, with chairman Sean Walsh saying at that time: 'There was no question of paying for a sub teacher or anything like that. Everything was totally above board. I accept that the way it appears in the book might give the impression that we paid him directly for missing time from teaching but there was never any question of the Kerry County Board breaking the GAA's rules on amateurism.'

Parsons made some interesting observations on amateurism himself.

'Maybe at some point the managers were volunteers and looked around on All-Ireland final day and felt, "I'm working as hard as that fella, yet he's being paid and I'm not. I need some level of compensation." It's a cancer if we define it as being a cancer. Maybe it's not. We pay 350 games development officers, they're paid professionals who coach kids, they're not volunteer coaches. What's the difference between paying them and paying a coach at inter-county level, with responsibilities for player development across the board? Is it fair to say that these coaches, who could give as much time as a coach that's paid by the GAA, are a cancer because they're being paid?'

The counter-argument is obvious. Though 'cancer' may be a dramatic term, it's wrong to pay managers under the counter – a widespread practice – because it's illegal, for one thing. Collecting cash by subterfuge and without paying tax is against the law, which means those who do so are criminals and are making fools of the other members of the GAA who are paying their taxes.

It's also against the rules of the GAA itself, which leads to some uncomfortable truths. If a county board is paying a manager under the table it's breaking the rules of the Association, which is bad enough, but the mess gets worse because part of a county board's job is to enforce those rules. It's surprising, in fact, that some rebellious county board delegate or other, furious at a punishment his club are facing, has not pointed out the hypocrisy at play here. How can one unit of an organisation (the county board) punish another (the club) for breaking rules when it (the board) is breaking a whole other set of rules?

Finally, the paid manager not only sets up an unnecessary tension in dressing rooms, between unpaid players and their paid boss, it contradicts the GAA's ethos on voluntarism and is a threat to the organisation's credibility. Proclaiming the value of volunteers in public is a tricky proposition when managers are being paid in secret. 'I agree,' said Parsons.

'It's the known unknowns – we know we're breaching the rules but as long as I don't know about it, we can get on with things. The concept of investing in games development, in good coaches who can educate players, that can only be good for player welfare. At the very minimum, make it transparent at senior level so that these fellas aren't paid coaches but paid development officers. Then their KPIs [key performance indicators] are more than winning at all costs. That's where amateur status needs to be open and transparent. Then you have the rates available, you can say to a manager, "We need you for thirty-five hours a week so for the sake of your sanity you can't work your main job, you'll have to change that to sign this contract."

'That way it's about player development and retention rather than just winning, and the whole shadow economy is gone. You can only have one All-Ireland winner, after all. Managers coming in and putting their profile as the priority, that's toxic. Unfortunately, even at club level there's nothing worse than an outside coach coming in who doesn't give a hoot about the club long-term but wants a win for his own profile. Yet at the end of the year even if the club is successful you might have four or five players with chronic hip issues because that manager ran them into the ground all year – to boost his own profile. That needs to be addressed and needs to be transparent. And people at the GAA's highest levels know and reports on the Association's amateur status have called for it to be transparent. The fear, though, is the ripple effect: will the players want to be paid?'

This is the flaw in the logic, and an error in reasoning one sees over and over in the GAA. If X occurs then Y will surely occur as a result. In this instance a vague concern about the possibility of player payment in the future shouldn't obstruct dealing with the reality of manager payment in the present.

In October 2024 GAA President Jarlath Burns asked the obvious question in an RTÉ interview, as quoted on page 75:

What does it mean to be a GAA inter-county player in 2024 and what does it mean to be a manager?

Anderson raised the obvious complicating factor: the introduction of contract and employment law for the professional managers of amateur players, but this is a complication that may have to be addressed. As Tom Parsons said, it can't be brushed under the carpet for the next ten years:

'You just can't. The transparency now is very important – cash is gone – so those known unknowns won't last. We're seeing audits of counties, and the GAA needs to be transparent. That fear – we'll pay managers so players will want to be paid – can be controlled if you engage with players and create an environment where they're happy to play. Then it doesn't matter if the manager is paid or not. In fact, players already know the managers are being paid, so transparency on the issue isn't going to change their minds on wanting to play for their counties.

'The era of turning a blind eye is over. We have to be transparent. When I call for the payment of managers it's not a betrayal of what the GAA stands for, I think it doubles down on what the GAA stands for. Voluntarism has to be appropriate for modern living. Giving ten hours of your time to coach a team, or to be on a club committee meeting twice a week, or being a player training twice a week . . . when you get into the realm of giving thirty or thirty-five hours a week, is it fair to expect voluntarism at that level?

'At inter-county level managers and coaches planning sessions, running sessions, analysing data, all of those things – is that the same as giving ten hours a week training fourteen-year-olds? Surely there's a barrier to voluntarism here and it's only fair and reasonable to compensate this person.'

PART 3
INTER-COUNTY

FOUR GREEN FIELDS AND
HOW THEY'RE ADMINISTERED

Where is the love for the provincial councils? You will hear GAA members grumble about Croke Park and froth at the mouth about their own county boards. They will vilify their own club officers and blacken the names of referees. But nothing seems to anger them like the provincial councils. Needless bureaucracy, a bar to progress, killing the open draw: nothing justifies their existence, and some of the more swivel-eyed observers suggest that abolishing them would solve all the problems of the Association in one fell swoop.

With that in mind I spoke to one of the ablest administrators in the GAA, Ger Ryan of the Munster Council, who started off by acknowledging that scepticism.

'One thing worth having a look at is our development plan, where we're coming from as a provincial council nowadays, because we would recognise that people are saying, "What's the benefit of provincial councils?" People are probably [asking], where do they really fit into the hierarchy? And I suppose we would see ourselves in a couple of different ways.

'Number one, we're a provider of games and organiser of championships locally, which is important. And wherever the provincial championships go . . . somebody needs to run them and to try to run those centrally would be virtually impossible. That's very important.

'The Munster senior hurling championship is the most important in terms of the amount of funding attendance it generates. In 2023, we had over 300,000 people, thanks to Cork this year [versus Limerick 2024, attendance 41,000], it's probably going to be over 300,000 for this year. That's a lot of bodies and it generates a lot of funding. And from a ticket pricing point of view people see value in it, if we put the prices up a fiver and that's a headline figure, it's twenty per cent. People might say that's not fair. But we feel we put that to good use.'

The provincial council's funding role is key, he added.

'The second thing is, we are a source of funds for clubs and countries. So for instance, at present we have a funding model that over the next three to five years, we will give €1.2 million to each county in order to fund activities. And that's beyond anything they'll get from central funds. Again, that's very important. We would want to support participation in particular because that's a growing challenge. That goes across all counties.

'We're not doing funding, then, that gives any county a competitive advantage over another. We're not saying we'll fund strength and conditioning – we'll fund facilities that increase participation and which focus on participation.

'We also have to try and help counties with stadiums; we have four big stadiums in the province and two smaller ones. Waterford is being developed, though we're not the major funders. In terms of Páirc Uí Chaoimh being a drain on us – it's not. Now, it and other stadiums are funded by a model at present where they get fifteen per cent of the gate receipts.'

Ryan articulated the specific challenge of the funding model:

'If you're Manchester United or Liverpool you get all the receipts. The counties don't. What we're saying now is this funding model is broken. It costs more to maintain those stadiums. Developing them at the start and enhancing them is a different debate, but certainly in order to run them we believe we can do more and come up with a better funding model because most of their funding doesn't come from Central Council games or local championship games; it comes from the crowds that we can generate – again, primarily for Munster senior hurling championship games. So that's a huge part of what we do as well. It's distributing and managing the development side. Other provinces do different things.'

The provinces depend on their own championships to generate funding. What about the argument that those championships can be uncompetitive? A one-sided provincial championship neither develops the game nor generates that much interest.

'We've had three different [provincial football] winners in recent years and also we had three counties in the quarter-finals recently. Now, two of them were beaten, but the point is, in the last twenty years, Limerick, Clare and Tipperary have all been strong at various stages. Limerick and Clare have been in provincial finals, Tipperary winning provincial championships at senior and underage, Waterford making a show this year.

'Take the club development grants. Again, nobody has built a hurling wall with what we give them but at the same time, we can go to clubs and say, "Here's five, ten, twenty thousand euro if you're spending one hundred thousand on land or whatever." It brings a bit of focus and discipline to development as well because your clubs have to adhere to structures. That's good in terms of governance and managing it.'

Games development is another provincial council focus, said Ryan.

'Our other big area is coaching and games activity. There's been a lot of debate in the GAA over this. And there's a new funding model. I started out when I was vice chairman saying, "We need a minimum of twenty additional staff here." Cork was particularly underserved in terms of trying to get roughly one person for ten clubs.

'The second thing we want to do there was change the focus away from just being schools but working in clubs as well, because ultimately the club is the centre of what we do. It's really important to have links with schools, but what we want is self-sufficiency in clubs, so that you're not depending on outside people to come in all the time. That raises the standards but also encourages participation because parents are more discerning nowadays. If the kids are not getting looked after properly, in the sense of everything being right in terms of preparation and governance and child safeguarding, but also in terms of the quality of coaching, parents won't be happy.

'It's raising that all up. That's very important. So we have fifty-four staff now, and they're much better distributed, and we can focus better. We have additional funding centrally, which is excellent, and we also add our own funding to that.'

Finding where the games need promotion is a challenge in itself. Ryan pointed out that the Munster Council identified six urban projects even though, as he said:

'There's a tendency to focus on rural depopulation, which is an absolute challenge for the GAA, but there are urban challenges also. We have lots of facilities in rural areas and the opposite in urban areas sometimes. The six projects are the northside of Cork; Clonmel, with a population of twenty thousand and five GAA pitches, while some rural clubs would have that amount of pitches to themselves; around Waterford city and Tramore; Limerick city; Listowel–Tralee in Kerry; and Shannon–Ennis in Clare. These are growing urban areas. Look at Tralee – it's done well in terms of senior teams but they may still have some challenges there.

'When you look at that I think there's a focus there that can come from a provincial council in terms of knowledge and local support that could get lost if we're looking at it centrally.'

This is a trump card for the provincial councils; they can claim to be closer to local issues than Croke Park and therefore use funding in a more targeted way.

'The other area where we can provide service is in terms of just literally being an administrative service provider to counties. We can help them run their finances better, we can help them run their HR – we employ lots of people but you wouldn't maybe justify having a full-time finance manager or full-time HR person in every county. We're agnostic there, though – what we do doesn't make Cork better than Kerry or Tipperary better than Clare.'

How difficult is it to stave off accusations of partisanship – 'This county's not managing its affairs properly but you're helping them, to our detriment'?

'It's a balancing act, but I think it's getting people to see that with certain things there's probably a good way to do something rather than six different ways to do it, and if we can, we help them get through it. To give an example, we have a finance manager in Munster, a very experienced guy, and he would work with counties and show them how best to structure and organise. That can mean simple things, like having better reporting. It's not money disappearing, it's how you manage any business, any bit of structure and manage cash flow. How you manage all of these things.

'The other thing is, as you know, there's been an HR review in the GAA, sort of how staff are managed and so on, so we can be part of that pyramid. If you take a bank, it wouldn't say it has everything centralised and doesn't know its regional structure. In Munster, and other provinces, you have the autonomy to make decisions, and I don't think it would make sense to run everything centrally. I think provinces have a good track record there, and counties like dealing with the provinces. They feel, "I'm understood, I don't have to explain it, I'm not dealing with somebody different every day." Then you can collaborate better together.'

That's maybe the most significant part of the provincial council's role. Organising Munster finals is the glitzy element, but for Ryan the fine print of service provision is crucial.

'The provincial councils need to be alert to that, particularly in the area around service provision, that that's where a lot of their future is. In our development plan. We have a role in discipline, which is an important part of the GAA's activities. We've appointed an Irish and cultural officer; it's a core part of our activities that makes sense at provincial level. The province is represented by the chair on National Management Committee, and on Central Council, and, you know, brings maybe a less partisan part to that in terms of governance.

'In addition to that, one of the challenges we really face is the whole volunteer area. I think we can help to a greater extent, maybe, in terms of training and providing assistance. There are multiple reasons why we can't get people involved, but one is availability of time. Another is that it becomes like a second job, and some people are ideally fit for that. Personally I'm in the finance sector, which is all governance, so this is something I'm used to. Developing pitches would be different!

'But while the roles are different, there's a lot involved now in terms of governance that wasn't there before. We're a little bit like the charity sector in that those rules are there, and sometimes the amount of governance we have to put on people, I think they can be quite scared of it. Scared that if something goes wrong you'll be held liable and look foolish. They can end up saying, "I actually don't enjoy this stuff; I just wanted to help my club."

'In terms of education, practical advice, support, provincial councils are playing a role there and continue to play a very positive role there, too.'

Perhaps the GAA would be better off without the provincial councils; perhaps it is a redundant layer of bureaucracy. But when Ryan identified key challenges to the GAA – compliance, voluntarism, urban depopulation – he made a strong case for a provincial council's agility in dealing with them. If it takes the overall view afforded by being outside a county but below Croke Park, the provincial council can be a powerful asset at all levels of the GAA. Who wouldn't want that?

GAA LAW: A SUITABLE CASE FOR TREATMENT

You don't have to be a fan of Manchester United to recall the team's Champions League semi-final against Juventus back in the 1998–99 season. That was the evening when Roy Keane, United's midfield dynamo, picked up the booking that would rule him out of the final. The Cork man shrugged off the disappointment to give an outstanding performance, scoring one goal and driving his teammates on from midfield. Much lauded by his manager Alex Ferguson, Keane's display was instrumental in getting his side to the final. And they duly won that final in dramatic style, when substitutes Teddy Sheringham and Ole Gunnar Solksjær beat Bayern Munich with two late, late goals. In the footage of the on-field celebrations afterwards Keane can be seen in his club suit, mixing with his clubmates, having missed out on probably the biggest game of his career.

The reason I mention this incident is not so much what happened as what didn't happen. Keane's yellow card was a run-of-the-mill decision for the referee; he lunged for the ball when a teammate's pass was slightly undercooked and caught an opponent, and there was no debate about the card. In the aftermath there was a general acknowledgement of the poignancy of the situation. Here was the player who had done most in the semi-final to help get the team through, but he'd miss out on the final.

What we didn't hear was a call for the suspension to be lifted or for the sanction to be challenged or for the player to be allowed to line out on grounds no more convincing than it wouldn't be fair for him to miss the game. In other words, there was no GAA-style appeal against a suspension that was entirely proportionate and reasonable.

The logic behind the GAA appeals system is perfectly sound in principle. Allowing players to look at a way to test the disciplinary process seems fair on the basis that any human system is open to the occasional mistake. Legal systems are by their nature open to interpretation, and decisions may be challenged on the basis of flawed process or various other grounds.

However, there is an alternative view, which is that the GAA cannot possibly be serious about its disciplinary processes when they can be circumvented so often. In the Roy Keane case there was never a chance that he would play in the next game in that competition, even if that next game was the biggest in all of Europe that season, a historic event. This is a routine occurrence in professional sport: players miss out on games through suspension all the time. If you watch enough soccer games on TV, at some point you'll hear the commentator say, 'That's a second yellow for X, he'll miss the next game.' What you will not hear is, 'All depending on how they get on at the appeals hearing next Wednesday evening, of course.' If this is the approach taken by professional sports, why is it different in GAA circles?

To be fair to Jack Anderson, he mounted a strong defence (and befitting a legal expert, quickly established the specific reason Keane was suspended):

'With Keane it was the accumulation of yellow cards, and not the semi-final card itself which was the problem, but I take your point.

'I think a more egregious example was the previous year [1998] and Laurent Blanc's red against Croatia in the World

Cup semi-final when Slaven Bilić went down as if shot by a sniper. It was a home World Cup and Blanc was a key, experienced player for France, he'd never been sent off before and the video evidence showed that it was pretty harmless, but there was no appeal. If it happened in GAA, there probably would have been some sort of appeal.'

Is it significant that the 'probably' is more or less superfluous in that sentence?

'I think that there are several reasons for the differences. First, for soccer, because they play so many games over a season, it's accepted almost as an occupational hazard that you will at some point miss games, and thus that culture of appealing is not so ingrained. In contrast, in the GAA there are so few Championship games that missing one may mean missing a quarter of the season, which means every match missed is so precious.

'Second, if you look at the GAA's history, we love a technical objection. In the past All-Ireland titles have been won and lost on objections, so it's almost a cultural thing, a bit like in the courts with driving offences . . . Moreover, every club or county seems to have a person who can divine a loophole by shaking his pen over the rulebook.

'Third, the rules of soccer are pretty clear, but traditionally the GAA rulebook was a bit vague, or internally inconsistent, so it was not that difficult for Rulebook Man to find some sort of technical procedural error.'

That said, even the great old sport of finding a name misspelt *as Gaeilge*, or paper with the wrong watermark or some of the other traditional ways of sidestepping a suspension, has to come to an end. Anderson pointed to a couple of cases that concentrated GAA minds. 'The high – or low – point for all of this was the Diarmuid Connolly appeal to the DRA [Disputes Resolution Authority] in 2015.'

Dublin footballer Connolly had been red-carded for striking an opponent in the All-Ireland semi-final against Mayo, which carried an automatic suspension. However, he was controversially cleared by the DRA of a one-match suspension in the early hours of the morning before the replay against Mayo.

'After that the GAA really looked at how it dealt with disciplinary matters procedurally and put in some really good, professional people to look at the rules and to sit on its central hearings and appeals committees.

'If you look at the stats in the director general's reports, the number of appeals has really fallen off. I think teams also know that a disciplinary saga – we are taking this all the way to the DRA – can be very distracting and the prime example is probably Waterford back in 2017. They had a disciplinary saga that year with Tadhg de Búrca [tug of a helmet] and when Conor Gleeson was sent off in the All-Ireland semi-final against Cork, they had a hearing but left it after that. Gleeson was a huge loss for them, but they moved on.'

Waterford have a pretty decent record in this regard. Famously, John Mullane chose not to contest his suspension after being red-carded in the 2004 Munster final, which ruled him out of Waterford's narrow defeat to Kilkenny in the subsequent All-Ireland semi-final that year. Would Mullane have tipped the balance Waterford's way? There's no way to answer that question, but it's clear that his decision was a striking vote of confidence in a system that often takes shellfire for its inconsistencies. It's equally clear that many counties would have gone to the eleventh hour and beyond to get a player of his significance eligible for such a game.

For his part Anderson freely conceded that, 'the rulebook is a bit of a mess, mainly because it tries to do too much, from the ethos of the GAA to disciplinary regulations, to club constitutions and so on.'

'The disciplinary regulations on matters like misconduct rules or appeals are just bewilderingly complicated. I sit on some local AFL tribunals and they have a relatively simple system in comparison. The GAA rulebook is a bit like that line from Dickens on the court system: "immense masses of papers of all shapes and no shapes, which the bearers staggered under". That being said, the GAA's internal disciplinary system is not at all as bad as made out and, for me, the CHC [Central Hearings Committee] and CAC [Central Appeals Committee] have been doing a very good job as of late. I do think that a full-time disciplinary unit, rather than the CCCC [Central Competitions Control Committee], would be better with match review officers or citing commissioners reviewing games.'

Well, that would bring to an end the alphabet soup of disciplinary bodies within the GAA. Individual officers ruling on issues within 24 hours of a game would be a far swifter and more efficient process.

Of course, it would also mean the end of some great stories, such as the one about a county board contacting one of the famous Rulebook Men mentioned by Jack Anderson because of a particular issue. The county's senior manager was looking for championship games to be postponed or some such; what were their options according to the rules? Rulebook Man explained what they could do. Earlier he had outlined to the senior manager in question what *his* options were.

For legal reasons, all parties must remain anonymous.

WHY WON'T PEOPLE PLAY THE GREATEST FIELD GAME IN THE WORLD?

At the conclusion of the 2024 inter-county hurling season, the GAA posted a brief video on its social media accounts of a few seconds' action from the All-I reland senior hurling final. The video showed Tony Kelly of Clare in dazzling form, collecting a pass and knifing through the Cork defence to flick home a superb goal from close range. 'There are moments in sport that bring time grinding to a halt, that bring us back to the very second we fell in love with the game,' read the accompanying text. 'Your @PwCIreland GAA/GPA HOTM on the biggest canvas of all, weaving his way through the red lines, flicking to the guarded net.'

True. There's no denying Kelly's brilliance, producing a game-changing score on the most important day of the hurling calendar, at the precise time when his team's need was greatest. The slow-motion video accentuates the touch and movement, giving viewers a fresh appreciation of the Clare man's skill.

And a fresh appreciation of the fact that he takes too many steps and fouls the ball.

This is not an indictment of Tony Kelly, whose quality is unquestioned. Neither is it a criticism of referee Johnny Murphy, whose umpires have a better view of Kelly's nine or ten steps with the ball and don't clock the overcarrying. And in fairness to all those officials, it's worth pointing out that, in the heat of battle, the Cork defenders bearing down on Kelly, who might have been expected to protest at the slightest possibility that the Clare star was overcarrying, made no great appeal for a free.

The point here is how informative that video clip is in a variety of different ways. What does it tell you about a sports organisation when its showcase action clip from the headline game of the year features an obvious breach of the rules? Is it reasonable to point out that this is just another example of hurling being a game that either won't or can't be officiated according to its official rules?

Perhaps it's a way to introduce a far more difficult question, one that hurling fans are reticent about acknowledging, let alone addressing. Why don't more people play hurling?

On the one hand their favourite sport is wildly entertaining and routinely serves up sinfully enjoyable matches; it's not unusual for a match to be consecrated as one of the greatest ever within hours of the final whistle, and such claims can often be made with plenty of supporting evidence. Thanks to scientific advances in conditioning, the modern player's touch and skill level is arguably higher than any of his predecessors', given the speed at which everything happens.

It's a rare season that doesn't offer at least a couple of highlights that defy belief and require quite a few slow-motion replays to be appreciated fully. And that dusty cliché about the Munster hurling final being one of the high holidays of modern Irish life is oddly stubborn; as one writer put it, the Munster final is one of the few events in Irish life that actually lives up to its billing.

A few years ago I was involved in making *The Game: The Story of Hurling*, a TV documentary series that aired to rapturous acclaim as viewers luxuriated in the stunning images and emotional narratives. It later helped secure special cultural status for hurling from UNESCO, a remarkable endorsement of the entertainment value of the game.

But all of that makes the question above even more pertinent: if it's that great why won't people play the game?

Everyone is familiar with the general theories. In centuries past hurling survived on good land but died out elsewhere, and its revival since then has proved just too difficult. The elite counties are more focused on their own internecine rivalries than on spreading the gospel. If you're not from an elite county you just don't have the innate ability to learn how to play hurling. The GAA centrally pays only lip service to the game compared to the slavish promotion of Gaelic football. If Dublin had won the All-Ireland hurling title in 1961 everything would be different. If Cork, Kilkenny and Tipperary focused on Gaelic football the whole thing would be far more competitive all round.

The theories get worse the longer you go on, but they're worth dismissing in reverse order.

Cork and, to a lesser extent, Tipperary are dual counties with a serious commitment to both codes and remain competitive in both. Although both have natural advantages in terms of size and population, their competitiveness is in fact a rebuke to other counties that focus almost exclusively on one code (almost always Gaelic football), but that's something to be discussed elsewhere. The counterfactual theory, in which Dublin use the 1961 hurling title as the springboard to become a superpower with the small ball, is an intriguing one. Tipperary won the game by one point ('The luckiest team ever to win that All-Ireland,' said Tipp midfielder Theo English decades later) but were the dominant team of the sixties anyway: one more title was hardly as significant as a Dublin victory might have been. But the issue with a counterfactual is just that: it's all theory.

Does the GAA centrally pay lip service to hurling? This is a more interesting line of inquiry. Every now and again there's a jarring misstep; a provincial council will post a list of training courses and omit hurling altogether, or a serious game is played on a surface unfit for rowdy bullocks, let alone a top-class hurling encounter. For instance, at the time of writing Galway and Tipperary had recently played out a National Hurling League (NHL) game in Salthill on an appalling surface, one so bad that it had an impact on the scoreline; Galway scored a late goal because a ball dropping in the square stuck in the turf rather than bouncing up into the Tipperary keeper's hand. Before this book was printed the NHL Division 2 final between Down and Kildare, a national decider, was played in Inniskeen, on a field with no 65-metre lines.

Finally, it should be pointed out that the general narrative about hurling can be pretty off-putting if one takes a step back. Claiming that a child needs to take up hurling when young if they're ever to master its skills, or that they should have a hurley in their hand all day to become a hurler, or that certain areas have natural hurlers or plenty of hurlers or always had plenty of natural hurlers . . . these are strange messages to give, particularly for a minority sport. Such bromides shroud hurling in an exclusive mystique and tell children that unless certain circumstances combine in their favour, they might not be able to play hurling. It may suit the hurling snob to see himself as a sporting cavalier, but in the end the cavaliers were undone by the roundheads. Yes, Gaelic football is the Oliver Cromwell-led side in this picture. That may be unfair, but it should be acknowledged that the games don't diverge sharply when it comes to their representation in lazy metaphors. Where they really diverge is in their treatment by the authorities.

At the time of writing a revolution had stirred in Gaelic football. Thanks to Jim Gavin's drive and leadership, the Football Review Committee (FRC) came up with some new rules which had the effect of improving the entertainment value of Gaelic football almost overnight. Three up and three back, the two-pointer, the solo-and-go: these initiatives became part of the jargon of the sport overnight. More to the point, they helped transform the sport into a far more enjoyable spectacle, and most important of all, they made the game more fun for players. The speed with which the GAA acted should be noted. President Jarlath Burns spoke about the FRC in February 2024 and within 12 months it had not only met enough times to come up with concrete proposals, it had introduced the most significant changes in the playing rules for decades. Those changes were badly needed: in the years beforehand the dreadful euphemisms had been deployed to describe the game, each of them a futile defence for a sport that was almost unwatchable (for more see the chapter on When GAA Rhetoric Goes Bad).

What did the GAA do for hurling in the same period? It appointed a new national head of hurling, Willie Maher. When the news broke, pundits such as Michael Duignan wished him well while noting how difficult his task was, given how little support hurling gets in certain parts of the country and how slow the GAA is to punish those working against hurling. At the time, Duignan told RTÉ:

> Sanctions in the GAA don't really work. They have never worked. The big thing here is the reality has to hit home. There are a lot of counties in this country that don't want hurling in their county. There are great hurling people in every county, but they are fighting an uphill battle. I don't want to name a county, but I am helping one of these counties in the background, they can't get their own county or province to support them in terms of what they are trying to do. There is

a group of them and they are hugely passionate. They need money, they need investment, they need new clubs.

Parity of esteem between the two sports, then? Hardly.

Does hurling need serious rules reform? The reflexive response from hurling pundits is usually along the lines of, 'You can't improve on perfection,' but hurling has a couple of issues. One is obvious – enforcement. The rules are there but aren't enforced. The other is less obvious; is the game just too fast for one referee?

Barry Kelly, the best hurling referee of the last twenty years, mulled over the changes in hurling.

'I finished inter-county refereeing five or six years ago and the game I refereed for nearly twenty years at that level was definitely a simpler game to referee. I did Tipperary–Galway's three semi-finals (2014, 2015, 2016) and they were all one-point games, all great games.

'There was an awful lot of what you could call "mano a mano" contests in those, but inter-county hurling has become an extremely difficult game to referee. Colm [Lyons] did an excellent job in the [2024] Munster final in the sense he got the balance right: how much do I let off and still maintain control?

'The game has changed so much, and that's without getting into issues such as legal and illegal hand passes, that the idea of what players do has changed. I'd have refereed Jackie Tyrrell a good bit – a top-class defender, but Jackie had a very simple approach that any reader can picture for him or herself. He'd get the ball, turn onto his left-hand side, and the nearest fella he'd hit would be Eoin Larkin seventy metres away. And he'd deliver the ball into the air, with Larkin expected to win his own possession and then maybe fire it over the bar. That kind of game is reasonably straightforward to referee. Now Barry Nash gets the ball and hand passes to William O'Donoghue, who gets the little flick pass to Declan Hannon who then eschews the obvious fifty-yard diagonal pass because he has Cian Lynch six yards in front of him waiting for the offload . . .

'That's not knocking Limerick, who are a phenomenal team, and every team is playing a version of that game now. It takes incredible skill and incredible discipline not to do what you probably learned to do at the club, which is to take a shot from seventy yards, but rather to pass the ball to one of the shooters. But there are so many collisions all over the field, the ball is moving so fast, so far . . .

'I would never have suggested two people referee a game because I always felt for the club administrators who would have to find twice as many referees. In Cork, for instance, where would you find all of those referees? But do you need two hurling referees now to keep up with the play? In football, iron-ically, it's nearly gone the opposite way. I think it was John Prenty in Connacht who was wondering about the obsession with strength conditioning when the majority of football teams are trying to avoid contact with opponents at all costs.'

The FRC mentioned earlier was manned by some of the most prominent Gaelic football personalities around: Gavin himself, Michael Murphy, Colm Collins, James Horan, Éamon Fitzmaurice. GAA President Burns said the organisation had 'hit the jackpot' in enlisting Gavin, but it also had a powerful advo-cate in Fitzmaurice, whose well-respected column in the *Examiner* and RTÉ commentary duties gave the committee platforms from which to spread the gospel of an improving game.

Even as the Gaelic football nation was basking in its new watchability, hurling was enduring its usual struggles, made no less difficult by their sheer predictability. In the approach to the

2025 Congress, Liam Griffin was proposing that every GAA club would field at least one hurling team from under-seven to under-ten level, just to give children the opportunity to play hurling. An even starker contrast with the FRC's exploits came in the shape of a motion from former Tipperary All-Ireland winner Conor O'Donovan. Having campaigned since 2018 for the GAA to stamp out thrown hand passes in hurling, he proposed that the transfer of the ball from the holding hand be prohibited, offering alternatives such as a pass from the non-holding hand or hand passing from either hand after it had first been bounced on the hurley. Griffin's motion was withdrawn; O'Donovan's was defeated.

(As an aside, it should be noted that even though it was taken as read that a rosy dawn was breaking for the sport of Gaelic football, the same Congress introduced a sixth different championship format in nine years. The new rules also required considerable 'enhancements' – i.e. corrections – which were delivered on the fly.)

The decisiveness with which Gaelic football was revamped and reshaped is welcome, though. Improving a sport is always a good move.

The question has to be asked, however: why can't that be done for hurling? The game is hardly going to grow if the units of the GAA charged with spreading it – county boards – are actively working to suppress hurling in their own areas.

Jack Anderson laughed when the issue came up.

'I've been involved in the GAA in Belfast and there were some people from certain counties who were more difficult to convince of the beauty of hurling than others, I'll put it like that.

'Look at it like this, about fifty years ago Title IX came into American sport, which ruled that women's college sports had to be on an equal footing with men's sports. You could introduce something similar in the GAA and tell county boards to bring in all Gaelic games and reward clubs which do that.

'A point some people have made is that there's no point in going to, say, the Tyrone County Board and telling them to do this or that with hurling; you're better off going to Carrickmore or one of the hurling clubs in that county and ask what can be done to help them. By that I mean rather than spreading the seed of hurling too widely, you go directly to where the green shoots are and you help them in every way you can. Take the Ards in Down or the clubs in Fermanagh; you try to grow it from there. Those clubs have to be given meaningful competition, and if that means crossing county boundaries, so be it. That was a point Martin Fogarty made more than once when he was the national hurling co-ordinator. The best unit in the GAA is the club unit, and it makes sense to help hurling at that level. I've seen cases where a county board has appointed a county hurling development officer, but that person has so much to do . . . instead, start where it's strong and build from there.

'You have to be real. A lot of areas in Ireland just have no interest in hurling and that's the way it is. There are different reasons, from the need for a lot of equipment compared to other sports, the need for good coaches to impart the basic skills, the slightly higher cost . . .'

And yet it can be done.

'It can be done. You see clubs in Dublin winning club All-Irelands, Slaughtneil in Derry, Naas in Kildare, they're all doing well. I'd love to see one of the leading counties competing for Liam MacCarthy "adopt" a weaker county – Limerick could take on Fermanagh, help those clubs and bring teams down for games, that kind of approach. If you're going to do all the talk about supporting the game then why not do so?

'And there's no consequence for counties who don't support or develop hurling either, don't forget. That's something that should be looked at in the future.'

This is a key element not just for hurling but for the GAA at large: the lack of consequences for simply opting out. When clubs and counties defraud the tax regime and undermine the GAA's own rules by paying managers with no punishment, it's no surprise that they act with impunity here. That's when you begin to notice that looking the other way with something awkward in one part of the Association can be echoed in another part.

The number of counties with realistic ambitions for an All-Ireland football title is pretty small – on a par with the number on the All-Ireland hurling title shortlist, to be honest – yet some of those counties seem content to focus their resources on Gaelic football anyway. If participation is the level of their potential in Gaelic football, why not just offer opportunities in participation for hurling too?

PART 4
MEDIA

THESE LADS HAVE TO GET UP FOR WORK
IN THE MORNING: TERRIBLE GAA RHETORIC

If the GAA is to further develop and flourish, something has to change in one specific area: The Department of Terrible GAA Rhetoric.

There are a couple of ways to look at the general calcification of GAA discourse. It should be acknowledged that no one sport has an exclusive distribution deal when it comes to terrible clichés, for one thing. That doesn't excuse some of the terrible GAA expressions, of course, but it offers some context. Every sport has its comfort blanket of meaningless boilerplate, comments or viewpoints which do no harm and perform something we learned about in sociolinguistics 101 long ago: they perform a phatic function in keeping the conversation rolling along without informing the discourse or advancing the debate.

Still, this is a considerable obstacle to improvement. If you're not expressing yourself clearly, how can you improve either as an individual or an organisation? Worse, if you're stuck in a rhetorical rut and unable to discuss matters without resorting to cliché, true development and growth remain out of reach. This is true in discussions of the games themselves, obviously.

There are basic offences beyond the ossified expression or the lazy description. In punditry, for instance, the use of 'we' is an obvious fault, one which presumably exists to show the closeness of the pundit to the county of origin (and shreds their credibility, but such is life). A friend of mine keeps a nickname index, in which he grades contributors on their fondness for nicknames.

But there are other issues which are more dangerous for the games.

Take one of the best examples – the He's Not That Kind Of Player defence. This is often used in hurling, though it's applicable to both codes. However, when a player strikes an opponent with a hurley, it's often defended by those discussing the incident on the grounds that the offending player didn't mean to make contact with his opponent's head/hand/groin, which means in turn that the foul is not as serious.

The logical conclusion is that it doesn't hurt as much when it's unintentional. A loose pull or flick that breaks a bone is, by this reasoning, harmless in comparison with a determined dunt delivered to a newly arrived substitute. Intention rather than force as a determining factor seems contrary to the principles of biology, and this bizarre side-step takes no account of the fact that someone has been struck with a three-foot length of timber. The analyst believes the guilty party was trying to play the ball, so logic dictates that he should be given a free pass when reefing a player's face open with a loose flick.

This is demonstrably untrue, of course. Still, the default position with apparently every pundit is that somehow the striking player should be cleared on the basis of assumed motivation – not a defence any court would entertain – and besides, he is 'not that kind of player'. Forget the fact that by striking an opponent he is showing that he most certainly is that kind of player. It's more important to point out that describing such a strike as one that deserves a serious sanction is not a character assassination; it is not going to follow that player around for ever.

Still, this is the level of much of our games-related discourse, where commentators are so shy of describing dangerous play as what it is that we end up with lukewarm descriptions and a good deal of both-sidesing.

Cases in point: as this book was going to print a weekend of the National Hurling League yielded a scatter of red cards, four in Kilkenny–Tipperary, three in Clare–Cork, which led to a good deal of discussion – though doublethink might be a better term – about head-high tackles. A few pundits acknowledged the danger of head-high tackles and the need for a zero-tolerance approach, but they still litigated individual incidents on a sliding scale of seriousness. It was a perfect illustration of what a zero-tolerance approach is not: the clue is in the 'zero'. Nobody seemed to acknowledge that if head-high tackles are to be eradicated all of them have to be punished by referees, a basic principle of deterrence lost as pundits reverted to type with players who didn't mean what they were doing and variations thereof.

This was also the time of the new football rules, which yielded high-scoring league games with plenty of free-running attacks and creative forward play. In the deserved praise for the new regime the old football discourse was also abandoned. No more intriguing or fascinating tactical battles (translation: sterility for observers, boredom for players), which had been the default description of Gaelic football in the dark years. Farewell, too, to the ultimate acknowledgement of a game too dull to watch: the arm-wrestle.

Other rhetorical flourishes are harder to eradicate. Both Gaelic football and hurling deploy He's Not That Kind Of Player, which is often closely followed by He'll Be Disappointed With Himself, which is fair enough until one considers someone else who'll Be Disappointed, by which I mean the opponent who may be getting several stitches in a gaping wound or have a broken jaw. Still, this is not as cringeworthy as He'll Have To Be Careful In Future. This is a baffling comment often used in punditry, apparently on the basis that it implies we have already moved beyond – far, far beyond – the incident being discussed. That event is already water under the bridge, so we must look to the future and through some sleight of hand or mind immediately forget the incident lately discussed. Related terms include a Coming Together for a violent clash or A Lot Going On for a series of violent off-the-ball clashes.

When you go deeper than these overused fall-backs, however, the discourse gets really interesting. For the purposes of illustration I need to refer to a disciplinary issue involving the former Kerry player Paul Galvin which happened back in 2010. This is not so much because of the inciting incident itself, which no one now recalls, or the way it was treated by the authorities (ditto) but the manner in which it was discussed. And the specific contributions of a couple of Galvin's fellow county men, none of which damaged the lazy cliché about Kerry people's talent for Jesuitical equivocation.

The most obvious place to start is the argument *ad hominem*, or the argument which is directed at the man rather than the issue. Or the ball. Shooting the messenger is the non-Latin phrase. At the time of the Galvin incident former Kerry player Darragh Ó Sé talked about the *Sunday Game* panellist Anthony Tohill's view of the incident rather than the incident itself.

'Anthony Tohill went on too much about it,' said Ó Sé. 'If Paul Galvin was man of the match, then he should have got the man of the match. He kept on going on about Paul Galvin not being in line for it because of that incident.'

Speaking to *Newstalk*, Ó Sé added that Tohill 'didn't have to be judge and jury on the whole thing. It wasn't his place to be in that situation and I just felt he should know better.' The former Kerry midfielder then moved on to a classic *argumentum ad consequentiam*, the fallacy where a proposition is deemed to be true because belief in it has good consequences for the person who is making that argument. 'I don't think Paul went out deliberately, there was just a bit of grappling and shoving,' Ó Sé said. 'To be fair to Eoin Cadogan, he didn't go down in a heap. He got on with it and I thought the referee dealt with it.'

Ó Sé wrapped up his radio interview with a version of the *argumentum ad ignorantiam*, wherein a speaker suggests that a proposition must be wrong because he or she is incapable of accepting that it might be true. 'In situations like that when people come close to pushing and shoving, it happens so fast and I don't think anyone in their right mind would put a finger in a guy's mouth,' said Ó Sé. 'It doesn't make sense.'

In a related newspaper interview, Ó Sé displayed his versatility with the *argumentum ad metum*, in which an orator attempts to build support for his views by creating an alternative scenario which most people would find unappealing. 'What a tragedy it would be for the GAA if they lost the likes of Paul,' Ó Sé told the newspaper. 'How entertaining would the championship be without a player like that?'

Ó Sé was joined on the airwaves by an all-time Kerry legend and all-round good egg, Mikey Sheehy, whose nimble footwork on the field of play was replicated by some dexterous oratory. Sheehy launched a classic *argumentum ad verecundiam*, appealing to a figure of authority as an infallible support for one's thesis. In this case, the referee, Pat McEnaney, was the figure of authority invoked. 'There was certainly pressure put on Pat McEnaney, there is no doubt he is the best referee in the game,' Sheehy told RTÉ's *Morning Ireland*. 'If Pat McEnaney was happy with what happened during the game, I felt it should have been left at that. He was quite close to the incident when it happened and it was difficult for him to make a call. His linesman was quite close to it and he didn't even deem it to warrant a yellow card.' (Sheehy was echoing the words of Jack O'Connor from earlier that week, when the Kerry manager said: 'I'm pretty sure he'll [Galvin] be okay, you have the best referee in the county looking at it from two yards away and there was a bit going on, on both sides.')

Finally, Sheehy gave an airing to one of the best-known fallacies, the *argumentum ad populum*, commonly used to convince one's audience that a belief that is widely held is true – in addition to being popular. In this case, the belief centred on Galvin being much maligned and victimised because of his past indiscretions. 'I suppose there was a bit of baggage from the National League game when both of them were sent off for a bit of a handbag incident,' said Sheehy. 'I think he is suffering because of previous misdemeanours, or so-called misdemeanours.'

Emphatic proof that either the art of elegant argument is alive and well and living in Kerry – not that we ever doubted it – or that debate on GAA issues needs to be clearer and more substantive. Take your pick.

In truth that's the fun part of terrible GAA rhetoric. It's slightly less entertaining when applied to one of the organisation's financial disasters, the €30 million debt on Páirc Uí Chaoimh.

The significance of this shambles is discussed in detail elsewhere in this book – the shadow it casts over the GAA's plans for infrastructural development everywhere, the damage done to the Association's financial credibility, the fixture problems for Cork – but it has also led to a curious sub-genre of outlandish business-oriented, or perhaps business-adjacent, justifications. For instance, the troubled Casement Park redevelopment saga has been repeatedly invoked as a semi-justification of Páirc Uí Chaoimh. This runs along the lines of 'Look how expensive

Casement Park is now and you have to accept that Páirc Uí Chaoimh was good value.' An impressive rationalisation.

It was counterbalanced by the approach to sponsorship revenue. When signing the stadium sponsorship deal with SuperValu a Cork GAA official said that 'any funding from such an arrangement will be used to help ensure that our games, from Rebel Óg to inter-county, continue to grow'. Yet if a debt is so crushingly large that all revenue streams had to be considered to pay it off, how could a particular revenue stream be diverted to buying hurleys and footballs?

SLOGANS ARE (NOT) FOREVER: MORE TERRIBLE GAA RHETORIC

In 2012 the GAA took a new approach in terms of marketing itself. At the time there was plenty of sport on the horizon. Ireland's men's soccer side were going to participate in the Euro 2012 finals, while the Olympics were due to take place next door in London, with plenty of athletes in green singlets taking part. With that kind of competition the GAA took the view that there was an angle in marketing itself by way of comparing hurling and football games to sports being played in faraway venues.

'We're telling the Irish public that we have the two best field games in the world – so don't miss them,' said the Ulster Council President of the time, Aogán Ó Fearghail, who in turn would become president of the GAA.

> TV is the competitor for us this summer, but you can't watch these games [the Euros and the Olympics] on the island of Ireland. There is sport taking place here and our new slogan has come about from within our own membership. When your own club or county is playing, how often do you hear someone saying 'it was great to be there' or 'I wouldn't have missed that'. Nothing beats being there.

It was a clever move, deploying the local and accessible against events which were harder to access, and it was grounded in logic: London and the Olympics mightn't be an unreachable destination, but how could it compare to something going on down the road? Furthermore, there was a subtle appeal that would warm the cockles of any GAA treasurer's heart. Go to the game and enjoy it in the flesh; that's the ultimate expression of your GAA membership and the sheer physical experience is the final validation. And the entry fee doesn't hurt when you're totting up the figures at the end of the year, either. Engaged crowds, good atmosphere, interacting with players: nothing beats being there.

Seven years later the GAA unveiled a different message, a mission statement in poster format designed to convey a sense of belonging – to clubs and the wider Association alike.

That mission statement read as follows:

We all belong in this place. We belong not because of who we are or where we come from, being here means belonging, belonging means knowing that you're part of a community that has a place for all, where potential is nurtured, where individuals become teams who honour the legacy of those who went before and strive to build legacy of their own.

Some of us play, some of us used to play, some of us never played.

We all belong, belonging means having a voice, means being able to say what you think is right being listened to.

The manifesto was soon shortened to be built around a simpler message – 'GAA – Where We All Belong'/'CLG – Tá Áit Dúinn Uilig Ann'.

The newer message was a generous one, aimed at welcoming people to the GAA and ensuring that everyone felt at home within the Association. It couldn't be faulted on the sentiment, certainly, and its message of inclusion was a timely one as the demographics of the country were changing significantly.

Could it be contrasted with 'Nothing beats being there' as carrying a slightly different message, though? It could certainly be argued that 'Where We All Belong' is better in one sense. The inclusion message is a step away from something that can be off-putting to many people who might otherwise be well disposed, or at least neutral, towards the GAA.

And that's the undercurrent with the GAA sometimes; having to reinforce its dominance, hinting that everything else in sport is subordinate, if not substantially inferior. By focusing on its openness, 'Where We All Belong' did some heavy lifting, indicating an openness that wasn't always apparent in the GAA's attitude in the past.

That was important because some of the challenges on the horizon demand that openness. Integration is the most obvious example, but developing a narrative of awareness and accept-ance of the need for more collaboration and co-operation is also important. And not just with other sporting bodies but also the various state and government agencies and local authorities the GAA has to work with. It's good to take the temperature and find an opposing view.

An alternative view of 'Where We All Belong' introduces a significant comparison, though. The 'belonging' isn't as con-crete a term as the last two words in the old motto. 'Nothing beats being there' is definite and specific, spelling out the neces-sity for the GAA member's physical presence. Can 'belonging' be a virtual commitment?

'What happened to the old slogan?' said Dara Ó Cinnéide. 'And not so old, either – "Nothing beats being there"?'

'I'm not for a second saying not to televise games, or to go back to the old days of just showing the All-Ireland semi-finals and finals on television, but we have gone the other way alto-gether. As Paddy Kavanagh said, "We have tested and tasted too much". It's a concern and a challenge. Press the button if you don't like it? That's not the GAA.'

'"Nothing beats being there" means you can bring your kids to a game, perhaps a county challenge game or a National League game, and they can walk out onto the field and shake hands or get a photo taken with their favourite player.

'That's a small thing and a big thing. You're roaring for them for an hour, and then you're talking to them face to face and they're still in their gear. That's the GAA.'

Small things and big things. In this case, as in many others, the small things can tell you a lot about the bigger things. GAA rhetoric sometimes tells us more than we might first imagine about the organisation.

CUE THE JAMES LAST THEME: IT'S SUMMERTIME

It's a phenomenon. There's just no other way to describe it. *The Sunday Game* has been a mainstay not just of RTÉ's scheduling, not just a cornerstone of Gaelic games, but a cliché come true: it's part of the Irish summer. An institution. From the terrible knitwear of the early years to Tomás Ó Sé's bow ties, from Joe Brolly's rants to Pat Spillane's one-liners, it has long been an integral part of Irish life. As soon as that unmistakable James Last theme starts, it's officially summertime.

Why do so many people have a problem with it, then?

One of the original sins for *The Sunday Game*, for instance, is that it doesn't cover everything equally. If your county is not challenging regularly for All-Ireland honours you might struggle to see it perform championship heroics on Sunday night.

An easy opener for the man who oversees RTÉ's sports output, which is part of far wider broadcasting obligations, as he points out, and not the same at all as overseeing a dedicated sports channel. Is it just too difficult to cover all the GAA games played on a busy summer weekend? 'It's not difficult,' says Declan McBennett, RTÉ's head of sport.

'It's impossible. Literally impossible. RTÉ entered into a rights negotiation a number of years ago but twelve months after that, the whole format of the championship was changed in terms of back doors, qualifiers, additional games. There are now a multiple of games compared to what there used to be.

There are round robin groups. There are knockout phases. There used to be straight knockout – go back to the great days of 1999, 1992, 1993 when Down and Derry and Donegal were knocking lumps out of each other, and the All-Ireland champions might be gone altogether in round one of the championship. Now there are so many games we've had to introduce a Saturday night highlights programme.'

The specifics? The disaffected fan from an unsuccessful county pipes up about his team, but there's a wider context. Like the future of the highlights-based programme in the first place.

'The two greatest criticisms of RTÉ for a decade or more were: number one, they're only there from May to September and number two, as you say, why can I only see twenty or thirty seconds of Carlow versus Laois in the first round of the Leinster Football Championship on a Sunday night? Why am I being treated differently to the big counties? Introducing more games was the answer to losing the All-Ireland champions the first day out, but that answer, in television terms, doesn't work.

'Let's take the two highlights programmes. Highlights programmes are dying in television terms. The two that survive are *Match of the Day*, which has a legacy in the UK, and *The Sunday Game*, which has a legacy in Irish terms. And both of them are arguably on the decline, because social media and digital have come in. You can now see clips from the match within seconds, in some cases, or minutes at most. So if Mo Salah scores a goal at 3.23 pm against Fulham, and the game is not on television, by 3.24 or 3.25 you'll be able to access clips of the goal on your phone through social media. So highlights are an issue there.

'But we've actually introduced more highlights programmes, which is a contradiction in itself, to try and establish the games. There are some weekends when there are twenty-one matches in the GAA calendar, yet there are other weekends when there are four. That doesn't make any sense. So we've adopted a policy whereby on the weekends where there are ten or more games we have a Saturday night highlights as well as a Sunday night highlights.

'But the criticism still exists. If I'm in one of the so-called weaker counties, if I'm in a Carlow or Laois or in Tipperary or Waterford in football and I see thirty seconds, do I feel vindicated in terms of what I'm trying to do at club level, what I'm trying to do at county level, trying to bring guys on? No, because all the glory is going to others. But the reality of it is the crowd at that game doesn't reflect the effort that's going in. And we're limited by having, in some cases, a two-hour programme for twenty-one games. It is impossible to satisfy everyone.'

Hence the choices that have to be made. The decision of which game to show first on Sunday night has a logic to it.

'We may be asked, "Why do you show the main game of the day as the first up?" Because there were forty thousand in Semple Stadium watching the game, and it was the game of the day. And if Liverpool play Man City, *Match of the Day* will start with Liverpool versus Man City: they will not start with Fulham versus Wolves, because people want to see the game of the day, the big moments of the day, the best players of the day, the biggest crowds of the day.

'I fully understand and I fully accept the criticism of "Why was the game I'm interested in only given thirty seconds?" What has RTÉ done to address that? We've shown more games than ever. If RTÉ do thirty-one games, plus the Tailteann and Joe McDonough and GAAGO do forty games, that's seventy games in the championship that are now covered, compared to the days when we were covering six.'

McBennett's reference to the person working hard at their club or in their county to promote Gaelic games is an interesting one. Because when it comes to Terrible GAA Rhetoric, RTÉ is often tarred with a particular scathing line when these matters are discussed, one which readers have probably heard at their own club or on the sidelines or in the pub, and which is usually delivered with the certainty of an argument-clencher. RTÉ Are Doing Nothing To Promote Our Games.

The reason for that is simple. That Is Not The Media's Job. 'It's not remotely our function,' says McBennett.

'The person who occupied this office before me was Ryle Nugent. Yeah, he was seen as the rugby guy. And because I came from Monaghan and, as they say, hockey and some other sports aren't big in Monaghan but my roots are in the GAA . . . I became the GAA man. But the reality of it is, I'm the head of sport. My job is to put sport on RTÉ. We have gone from six hundred hours of sport to one thousand hours of sport. We've done more women's sport than we've ever done before, athletics, rowing, gymnastics, the global sports that we now compete at. There's more GAA than there has ever been on the television. There is more Irish soccer than there has ever been on the television, and there is more rugby than there has ever been on the television.

'But everybody looks at it through their own prism. I saw one scribe complaining that we don't do enough on the club championship, so what are we paying our licence fee for? For the Olympics, for the Paralympics, for the Euros, for the GAA championship, for the rowing, the swimming. We're not a GAA station. We're not a soccer station. We're not a rugby station. We are a national broadcaster that covers sport. We're not even a sports station, but eaten bread is soon forgotten.'

McBennett warms to his theme:

'I smile at times at the new world that we live in, where there are so many podcasts and outlets where so many people who are able to have an opinion on GAA, people who are making a living off the back of the work that we are doing because we cover the games, and then they cover the games because we've covered the games.

'I did a lot of work with Joe Kernan and Armagh back in 2005–2006, and when I met him recently I quoted something back to him that he said back then. In 2005 he said, "Declan, the best thing about the GAA is that everybody owns it, and they have a sense of ownership of it; and the worst thing about the GAA is that everybody thinks they can have an opinion on the GAA, regardless of how uninformed or ill-informed it is." It's as relevant now, and it came up recently around the football rules debates. It's stuck with me for twenty years now, whereby everybody, and that is the beauty of the GAA, has a sense of ownership of it. It is in our DNA, and we feel deeply passionate about it.

'That doesn't mean it's the only sport out there, and it doesn't mean my county is the only county, and it doesn't mean that my view is the only view. But there are those who would tell you that no matter how many games you do, it's not enough. No matter what coverage you provide, it's not enough. No matter what level of criticism there is, there's not enough.'

McBennett's point about being seen as 'the GAA man' is worth dwelling on but not for the obvious reason. However he may be perceived by those who follow other sports, that description is no shield when it comes to bruising discussions with GAA officials and managers; in fact, the paranoia runs so deep with some of those individuals that, well . . .

'There are county managers who would tell you that RTÉ has a particular agenda for a county or against a county. I have

been accused of being somewhat sympathetic to those counties who are financially well off. This is the level of paranoia
that you're dealing with. Our job is to show the games, lads,
at the end of the day. We don't influence who wins the All-
Ireland, and to an extent, we don't care who wins the
All-Ireland, because whether it's Kerry, Dublin, Galway, Cork,
Limerick, whoever it happens to be doesn't make a difference
to us. What makes a difference to us is that the people who
watch our coverage have a sense that we did our level best to
cover the games.'

Which brings us to another obvious question. If there are
21 games being played on a weekend, what kind of staffing
levels and effort is required to do one's level best to cover
those games?

'On the weekends where you're covering that many games,
you have well over a hundred personnel working across the
board. The games are largely produced by TVM out of east
Cork, but we would have ten sub-editors here working on a
Sunday night because the games are coming in.

'We used to have a scenario in the past whereby the game
would be in Portlaoise, say, and somebody would get into the
car in Portlaoise and drive the tape back here. Now the technology allows us to get the game coming in directly. A pundit like
Tomás Ó Sé will be here at eleven o'clock in the morning
watching games, and he'll still be here at eleven o'clock that
night on *The Sunday Game*.

'Equally, when you get down to All-Ireland semi-final, final
level we have massive OBs [outside broadcasts], again you're
talking over a hundred people. It's a phenomenal demand and
it's a beast that only grows. Now we're in a privileged position
to do that. We never, ever take that privilege for granted nor
should we.

'But again, nobody outside the four walls has a clear under-standing as to what is required for us to get the personnel. You don't just phone somebody on a Sunday and say, "Will you be in Páirc Uí Chaoimh for half one? We're doing the Munster championship match."

'Yeah, it's a beast that eats and eats and eats and it has to be fed.'

CUE THE JAMES BOND THEME:
SUNDAY GAME CONSPIRACY THEORIES

The shadow cast by *The Sunday Game* is a long one, and it isn't always appreciated by those it falls upon. A common complaint among teams is the programme's focus on disciplinary issues, with a widespread belief that certain things happen if the pundits start examining all the camera angles and shots presented to them. To be fair, those angles are more freely available at 10 p.m. on a Sunday than in the white heat of a championship game, when a referee is trying to decipher a tangle of arms and legs forty metres away. The 'certain things' mentioned generally include the gears of the GAA's disciplinary machinery cranking into action to impose retrospective punishment on some player or other for either a harmless bump (his manager's view) or a shocking assault (his opponent's perspective).

Of course, Ireland being Ireland, this sometimes tips into full-blown paranoia. This pundit is known to be against this county, or that, or that commentator has never given us a break. This one? Black against our crowd. That one? Bitter, bitter, bitter. These are biases that are attributed to media figures in every sport and every country, of course. For most observers the only way Ireland is 'worse' is in the relatively small pool of pundits. The perceived enmities and vendettas ascribed to pundits are unsurprising insofar as those pundits have probably been embroiled in bitter rivalries with a couple of the counties who pop up regularly for analysis.

In hurling, for instance, the small number of competitive counties means that pundits with any level of credibility in the game have had lengthy playing careers themselves. And that in turn means many repeated encounters with the relatively few teams being analysed not to mention tours of duty on the coaching circuit in what once were opposing counties. If anything, this leads to renewed charges of bias because if he was coaching a club in county X which has a bitter rivalry with club Y, then he'll criticise the latter's county representatives but not the lads he managed himself . . . this way leads only to madness, of course, but it bumps up against a common refrain. Namely, that pundits wield undue influence over the GAA's disciplinary process, and by highlighting certain incidents they can drive the disciplinary agenda.

Their boss doesn't agree.

'To be honest, I don't view it as that, and if I did, there's two ways to address that,' said Declan McBennett. The job with the pundits or the analysts or the presenters or anybody involved in *The Sunday Game* is to analyse the game. If they're not analysing the games, they're not doing their job. So you can't analyse the games and not give a forthright opinion. The accusation has been that the opinions are not sufficiently forthright nowadays, despite the fact that we kind of insist that they're grounded in some sort of factual basis, which wasn't always the case.

'Let's face it, if you're going to do the job properly, then you have to analyse. They are not judge, jury or executioner. And if the GAA is that easily influenced, and the disciplinary process is that easily influenced by one single individual TV programme, then there's an issue at the heart of the GAA rulebook or the disciplinary process.

'If the GAA wanted to change that, they could have a citing commissioner in the morning and adopt the rugby model and say anybody who's caught on video evidence will face action. The commissioner could access the RTÉ footage or the GAAGO footage, or their own footage, consider it on Monday and a penalty is imposed.

'Now, what is RTÉ or *The Sunday Game* to do? If it stops doing its basic function of analysing the games, that immediately discredits it as a programme in itself. At that rate we might as well do what others do, which is run the highlights and have no analysis.'

Fair point. There's another twist to being a small community in a small country, however. People are always able to get in touch.

In his autobiography, Kerry great Pat Spillane deals with an urban legend that surfaces from time to time. The whisper that managers are happy to lean on pundits to get them to soft-pedal a player's misbehaviour. Spillane, characteristically forthright, puts his cards on the table.

The only time I was ever influenced in any way to do something on *The Sunday Game* was the incident when Paul Galvin threw a water bottle after an Armagh man back in 2006 after a few of them got tangled together by the Hogan Stand. Jack [O'Connor] was manager.

A person in the Kerry camp at the time rang me in the evening – this was the time I was presenting the programme rather than being a pundit, though. He asked me how we were dealing with the incident and I checked with the panel. They were quite adamant that Galvin was out of order and the incident would have to be dealt with on TV (as far as I can remember there was actually a photograph later of the water bottle hitting somebody in the crowd).

Fair enough. I was the presenter, the man who was asking the questions, and when the clip came on God knows it didn't make for good viewing. At all. But by a stroke of luck the clip also showed Armagh water carrier arriving to get involved in the shenanigans, so when he came onto the field in the clip, just as the panellists were warming up to discuss Galvin's behaviour, I said, 'And look at the water carrier!'

They started talking about the water carrier and more or less forgot about Galvin . . . It was the only time that I would say I was biased. I didn't deliberately intervene and say 'Look, he's innocent,' I deflected the lads to talk about something else, but it was wrong.

Pundit performance can also be analysed another way. If you are from county X and your star forward is obliterated by a defender from county Y you may tune in to *The Sunday Game* to see just how bad the tackle was and to hear calls for justice . . . only to see that the pundit dealing with the incident is from county Y.

McBennett acknowledges that it's a situation that can get sticky.

'I can tell you the players and the pundits who couldn't call out their own counties, not the RTÉ presenters.

'I've had an inter-county manager and an inter-county management backroom team indicate to me that it was their sense that we were somehow under the influence of those teams who were financially well off.

'If you go back to controversies around *The Sunday Game* in my tenure, Henry Shefflin and Jackie Tyrrell when Richie Hogan got sent off, Joe Brolly and Ciarán Whelan when Johnny Cooper got sent off, Paul Flynn after the All-Ireland final, when Mick Fitzsimons "put David Clifford in his pocket" (but he didn't) – those are the cases.

'There are former players and managers who couldn't address their own counties. And that brings up the question of whether the pundits should be on matches involving their own counties, but they are. They are given a role and told to do their job.'

Again, the size of the talent pool has some influence here. There are only so many people with the credibility to pronounce on the top games, and if that credibility comes from success with the county, then it's inevitable that successful players will end up discussing their own (successful) county.

Sometimes that's not enough – for the pundit themselves. Unsurprisingly, Dara Ó Cinnéide articulated the view from the other side of the desk better than anyone.

'I'd get upset enough, to be honest, listening to some pundits criticising football, a game I love. Fellas making money off the game. And I acknowledge absolutely I did the same myself, you have – we've all earned money with our opinions on the games. But somewhere in there we need to have respect for the game, for the lads who play the game and the people who train and manage them. I don't have an issue with people criticising the mother ship, the GAA itself, when it deserves to be criticised, but the USP for a few people seems to just be to be critical of the GAA and the games.

'I quit *The Sunday Game* because after three years or so I felt, "I don't really believe in this any more." I thought there'd be more of a reverence for the game itself, that it was bigger than lads dressing in nice suits and chatting about their golf handicap or the Galway Races. I felt outside the loop when I was on *The Sunday Game*.

'They're all good lads, I certainly couldn't say, "This fella is no good" or anything, but I didn't believe in being part of it. If someone said, "I saw what you said on *The Sunday Game* the other night." I'd be saying, "I only answered whatever question I was asked." I can remember having those conversations with the lads on *The Sunday Game*, that I wasn't feeling it. That said, I'd be disappointed in myself as well. I'd admit I didn't have the maturity for it. I should have said, for instance, "Paul Galvin slapped the notebook out of a referee's hand, we'll get over it."

'The final straw for me came when I had to acknowledge that I couldn't not be a Kerry person, if that makes sense. Kerry were successful when I was on the show so I was commenting on them a good bit and probably criticising them very little, probably less than I should have been. And I just didn't want to be part of that.

'When I went to TG4 I felt more able to drive the conversation more and that that conversation was less about some fella being sent off or not being sent off.'

Back in Montrose, there are other aspects of presenting and punditry worth looking at. Readers who scour Instagram will see that RTÉ presenters and commentators are available for master of ceremonies duties, for instance, across a wide range of sports.

That makes sense. A sports organisation investing thousands of euros in running a launch or formal event is obviously going to want an experienced, professional host for the night. And once again, the small media ecosystem in Ireland means that those with the requisite experience are often well known in other arenas. Such as broadcast media. This matter surfaced in relation to the firestorm of criticism RTÉ faced in the wake of the Ryan Tubridy controversy in 2024, when many of the external activities and deals that staff were engaged in came under the microscope.

Another way of looking at these arrangements has less to do with tax compliance and more to do with sports, however. How can a journalist report fairly on a sports organisation which is also paying that journalist for various gigs and events? Even sports reporters, who are usually accustomed to talking about games and players and scorelines, eventually have to ask some hard questions of an athlete, a manager or, more likely, a sports organisation. Is it appropriate to also be employed, even occasionally, by that organisation?

McBennett offers a stout defence:

'My honest response to that would be, show me the case where it did happen. Show me the case where it did. If Marty Morrissey is down and presents a bunch of medals to the under-twelves or he goes and he does the All-Ireland medal presentation, or Darragh Maloney or Joanne Cantwell does it, are they in the pocket of the team that they went to? Never once in my six years has it come up that RTÉ's impartiality was questioned because somebody was handing out medals or doing an MC or doing a gig. Should we isolate ourselves from the very people that we're trying to serve? Or should we be part of that?

'To my mind, we should be part of it until the day that it compromises our impartiality or our objectivity. Then, if that's on my watch, it's for me to address. But let that manager come to me and say, show me the example. It's a siege mentality, and I absolutely get it, and it has served many managers well, many of them from my own province.

'I have had complaints from two counties that I can think of whereby they were unhappy with our coverage. One was in relation to an off-the-cuff comment about the standard of facilities in a particular county, and the other was in terms of a siege mentality in the North. But no inter-county manager has ever lifted the phone and given me a piece of their mind – and good luck to them when they do, because if they have a legitimate point, fine, but they better be coming with a legitimate point.'

Fair enough. Whether that rebuts the *perception* of bias is another day's work, but it diverts us along yet another interesting side road: the GAA's relationship with the media as a whole.

Which is appalling.

HOW THE GAA'S ATTITUDE TO THE MEDIA UNDERMINES AMATEURISM

Early in 2025 GAA President Jarlath Burns included this section in his address to Congress.

> I also intend to work with our counties in the coming weeks to tackle the challenges we continue to experience in working with our managers and players to promote our games via media engagement.
>
> To provide one drastic example, in the two-week period before last year's two All-Ireland hurling semi-finals, not one interview was conducted with a national media outlet. Notwithstanding the demands on all of those involved with county teams, we cannot complain about airtime and print space afforded to our codes if we do not facilitate it. To those counties who do, I acknowledge and thank you for that.
>
> We don't always like the media attention that we get. It comes with the territory of being an organisation of our size and social importance that we are held to account, have a mirror held up to us and our performance is critiqued. But I can say that we are lucky to have the people who are the main correspondents covering our games, the vast majority of whom are active in their local clubs.
>
> We should not expect to be served by cheerleaders, and we have an authentic group who deserve our thanks and also an acknowledgement that we do not always help you, the media.

Under a proposed new arrangement, access to post-finals team holiday funding will be linked to measured media access around the national launches of our All-Ireland championships and games in the knockout phases of our All-Ireland series.

Burns wasn't exaggerating. This is John Fogarty in the *Examiner* the week of the Munster hurling final in 2024:

For the second year in a row, there will be no pre-match media conference before the provincial finals. Come to think of it, we can't remember Kilkenny ever doing media before a Leinster final and this is their seventh in a row, their 10th in 11 seasons. . . .

In Dublin's first Leinster final in three years and only their second in 11, the appearance is a gilt-edged opportunity to introduce people to this relatively new team of Micheál Donoghue's team. But no, the attitude is 'they can't be having that. Sure, won't beating Kilkenny speak for itself?'

This week, a player of the month event was due to take place. Nominees for May included Limerick's Cathal O'Neill and Dublin's Chris Crummey. However, word came through on Friday that it had been postponed.

By our count, it's at least the sixth time either this has happened or one player hasn't been available since the inception of the awards. We can only presume the reason is game-related.

Managers' fears about players saying the wrong thing when they are the best educated generation is plain paranoia. A chinwag the week of a game has done Gearóid Hegarty no harm in the past or Shane O'Donnell this year. Last month, the Clare star spoke the week of the Waterford game having received the award for April and delivered in Ennis five days later.

As Fogarty pointed out elsewhere in the column, tears for the journalists are unnecessary. The column inches will still get filled. The players just don't figure in those columns.

The GAA's relationship with the media is often linked directly to the marketing of its games, and the traditional viewpoint here is that hurlers are less marketable than footballers because of the headgear hurlers wear. The truth is actually far less nuanced. The reality is that GAA players are not marketed at all. Managers have shut down access to inter-county players to the extent that they are now seen almost entirely at sponsored/partnership gigs. Readers will notice that many lengthy feature interviews with GAA stars carry a footnote if in print (*Johnny Murphy is an ambassador for Oily Diesel Coffee) or a ghastly branded polo shirt if on video.

The sole exception is usually an All-Ireland final, at which some participants may be rustled up to talk to the Fourth Estate. 'Participant' is doing some heavy lifting when it comes to such events: it's not uncommon to go to one of those press calls and find a player who is either injured or so far down the pecking order he'll only appear if a meteorite obliterates the bus carrying the first 15.

Declan McBennett didn't beat around the bush when I mentioned this.

'I go back to Lar Corbett giving an interview which ran in the Sunday papers the day he got three goals in an All-Ireland final. It didn't affect his performance one iota.

'The siege mentality, particularly with county managers, is beyond sense. I'll give you a very, very simple example. The managers of the two teams in the All-Ireland finals should be in

Dublin on the Tuesday beforehand naming their teams, and that's as simple and straightforward as you could get. The level of dummy teams, the level of county board secrecy that's at play, it's outrageous, and we're all complicit here because we can't afford to say no because the other side or the other guy will get inside us and report it instead of us.

'I watch the NFL [American football] and if you're playing Kansas you know Patrick Mahomes is going to play against you. It's not a secret. It's not a secret David Clifford is going to play for Kerry every single week either. And if you can't figure out the tactics, the formation, or you can't have enough trust in your own players . . . We're all complicit, and it's gone to an outrageous level. And they hide. They systematically hide behind amateurism.

'I'm a Liverpool fan. The other night Rio Ferdinand was standing pitchside when Jude Bellingham was coming out of one dressing room and Mo Salah was coming out of the other. Compare that to here. We have to use media facilities here which are a disgrace. But then they're a disgrace across all sports.'

McBennett is correct about the GAA's media facilities. Before I left the sports beat it was becoming more and more common for the (often decrepit) press boxes of our GAA venues to be invaded by teams' backroom helpers: stats men and the like. More than one of those backroom men expressed disbelief at the standard of those press facilities.

Readers may have a short attention span when it comes to journalists' complaints about their seating arrangements or sightlines, particularly when those journalists are being paid to attend games. But the GAA's general misunderstanding of its relationship with the media is one that works against its own ends. For instance, the fact that county managers are the tail wagging the GAA dog means the games get less and less publicity. Allowing managers to lock their players away from interviews for the playing season has consequences. The GAA as a whole falls behind in the battle for hearts and minds, with its biggest stars mysterious, distant figures, unknown to the public, their personalities hidden, obscure, secret. In the case of hurling, its most famous practitioners spend their entire playing careers in a literal mask, while off the field they're sequestered away from the coverage that might spread their sporting gospel.

An obvious starting point here is springtime, when the GAA's national leagues begin at around the same time as the Six Nations. The leagues are competitions with an inbuilt competitiveness because of the way the divisions are organised, and GAA supporters are eager to get out of the house for a game or two after the winter; the smaller crowds ensure you can get tickets at your local venue . . . Yet these competitions erupt without any build-up, and the furtiveness seeps in everywhere. Counties don't announce teams or announce laughably inaccurate teams. The people who could market the games most effectively – the players – are nowhere to be found in the media. By contrast, at around the same time in the year, Irish rugby players are presented to the public, in the build-up to each game in the Six Nations, in all their infinite variety.

A simple comparison was made some years ago at a hurling development meeting in Croke Park, when it was pointed out that a 19-year-old making his debut for Ireland in the Six Nations would be the main feature of a press call the week of that game, would feature on TV and in every media outlet, driving interest in the event. By contrast, a 19-year-old making his debut in a national league game, hurling or football, in front of a couple of thousand hardy addicts, wouldn't see a Dictaphone for a couple of years. His manager would be apoplectic at the prospect of his young charge featuring in the media, but in real terms his blood pressure would be safe enough. No journalist would waste their time on a call or text inquiring about availability, such is the level of paranoia within the GAA.

The immediate retort, that the latter is an amateur and the rugby player a professional, falls to pieces immediately. First, that should make the GAA more, not less, proactive in getting players to promote the games. The rugby player is contractually obliged to carry out press duties, and the freedom to make time to do so; he therefore enjoys certain advantages in publicity terms. As a consequence the GAA centrally, and locally, should work harder to ensure its players are more prominent. Acknowledging the difference in the two athletes' status shouldn't be presented as an admission of defeat; it should be a spur to do more to redress the imbalance.

When it comes to publicising games the players are key. They're the ones who encourage kids to head out to the back garden or the road to try the same moves, flicks and shots. Those kids tend not to evaluate their role models on the basis that 'one is an amateur, one a professional'. Visibility doesn't come with a caveat when you're trying to market your sport.

That was one reason I spoke to marketing expert Shane O'Leary about the harm done to the GAA by keeping players shut away from the media. He started by torpedoing an idle thought I had, that the GAA could enjoy its own *Drive to Survive*-type breakout documentary series on a well-known streaming service.

'The point you make about a Netflix documentary – that's a fantastic way to tell stories but realistically, how many teams are going to give that access behind the scenes for a year? I don't think there's too many. Even though you've seen some of the biggest franchises do it – your Manchester Citys and so on

– they know the value of being able to tell stories, yet ironically, county boards don't understand the value of that and haven't gotten around to that.'

This is the big obstacle to that kind of documentary being made. It's inconceivable that a county manager would allow a camera crew to capture what he and his team are doing.

It should also be pointed out that wildly successful though *Drive To Survive* is, it's also sponsored content, essentially (sponcon, in the terminology of the business) a sleek, frictionless form of advertising designed to maximise profits for the company featured. It has achieved that goal with F1 in spectacular fashion, driving interest in the sport among demographics which the motor racing industry is interested in cultivating, not to mention the soaring interest in the United States, with an accompanying spike in the price of TV rights.

If a county side were willing to take the plunge, would it also enjoy a boost to its general visibility and bank account? Or would the audience reject an overt attempt at monetising a county jersey?

O'Leary pointed at the essential motivation of the big streaming companies:

'The likes of Amazon and Netflix, they only really care about themselves and have absolutely no empathy or understanding or knowledge of sports. And you might say, "Well, every broadcaster has that attitude," but I don't think that's really true, to be fair. I do think within RTÉ, Virgin, TG4 actually, there is a sense of a mutual understanding. "We have the games on but also we're investing in something that is an Irish pastime and tradition, and that means more to us than just the marketing perspective."

'Amazon and Netflix only really care about the number of subscribers and not really about the sport. Is it ever going to be realistic for them to invest in GAA to the right level that they will have either a scale or critical mass using their platform? I don't think that's ever going to be seen, really.

'In some jurisdictions where a TNT or Sky, for example, have invested heavily, the second that it becomes non-viable or their business changes, they drop those sports. I don't think it's feasible for one of them to come in just because of the economics at play. And is it viable for the GAA to have that?

'It may be advisable to have another broadcast bidder, which we don't have, but I don't know whether in the long term that would be a good move for the GAA or for any party.'

There's another philosophical difference here worth considering. If a GAA player is an amateur, should they accept money from a company to endorse its products? If they do, are they no longer an amateur and therefore unable to fend off the depredations of the media with their trusty shield of amateurism?

The 'these lads have to get up for work in the morning' argument is a good example of GAA Rhetoric Gone Bad, and it's explored at length elsewhere in this book, but there are awkward contradictions that present themselves here immediately when the 'getting up for work' argument is introduced.

First things first: a multinational corporation, or even a neighbourhood business, seeking to use a GAA player for publicity purposes should pay for that privilege. That goes without saying. Up to a few years ago there was a hierarchy when it came to sportspeople and endorsements which heavily favoured professional athletes in international sports, which was itself entirely understandable.

Nowadays high-profile GAA players can enjoy lucrative sponsorship deals and ambassadorships worth thousands of euros. It would be a rare member of the GAA who would begrudge them that perk, if only on the grounds of basic equity.

If a hurler or footballer is endorsing a product or appearing in an advertisement alongside a rugby or soccer international, surely the former is entitled to the same consideration as the latter? The answer has to be yes, as anything else would have a nasty smack of exploitation to it. However, the arrangement raises some awkward questions. Is the GAA player really an amateur any more if they are being paid for their image or endorsement? There is no hint of pay for play, but profiting from your proficiency can be interpreted as undermining your amateurism without confirming your professionalism.

There is yet another angle to these deals which is equally awkward. These product launches, announcements, press calls and photo shoots are usually accompanied by media access to the players concerned; these are usually soul-destroying meet-and-greets at which players lob out a few clichés and all the participants die a little bit inside.

Sometimes there's a bit of entertainment at these press side gigs. There was the time a GAA star claimed with exquisite disingenuousness at a sponsorship launch that he thought the photo shoot was 'vision only'. He had to be reminded by PR handlers that, predictable as they might be, the boilerplate comments were still expected from him. Then there was the sportswear announcement at which two rugby internationals simply jumped into a taxi to avoid speaking to the press, though presumably they cashed the cheques. However, if a hurler or footballer who is normally off limits to the press can speak freely at these gigs, does that mean he's happy to engage with the media as long as he's being paid?

This is tricky, because it deals a fatal blow to the argument that GAA players and professionals should be treated differently. And it folds the two groups together, with all that that entails.

MUTE INGLORIOUS MILTONS?
COUNTY PLAYERS SPEAK

The notion that inter-county players can't be trusted to speak to the media isn't just misguided: it's clearly incorrect. As a manifestation of control-freakery on the part of insecure managers it can't be beaten, of course. What a manager is saying is that while he expects a bright, capable young man to make split-second decisions in front of eighty thousand people when he's at the point of exhaustion after almost eighty minutes of hand-to-hand combat, he doesn't trust that same young man when he's faced by a microphone. The 'media ban', which is now the default setting for practically every county, also operates against a guiding principle of the GAA. If the organisation reflects the communities it represents, then surely it reflects those communities' concerns and challenges?

Where this gets uncomfortable is in the GAA's tacit support for campaigns such as the Hand on Heart campaign in the south-east of the country some years ago. In 2017 teams including Tipperary, Wexford, Waterford and Kilkenny joined the campaign, which highlighted the lack of 24/7 cardiac care in the south-east region and sought a second cath lab at University Hospital Waterford with the provision of 24-hour cardiac care for the region. As part of the campaign players, management and supporters placed their hands on their hearts at the playing of the national anthem at NHL games. It would take a pretty tone-deaf official to object to such a show of support, but the campaign also raised an interesting question. How many other, similar campaigns are missing out on the involvement of Gaelic games stars?

Over the years the odd glimpse of players' personalities has broken through their managers' imposition of North Korea-level firewalls. It's notable that that's often on issues of the day.

In March 2024 Mayo defender Pádraig O'Hora was critical of alcohol companies promoting alcohol-free products at sports events. O'Hora, who was working with Youth Work Ireland and the Mayo Mental Heath Association, expressed his concerns on RTÉ's *Up Front* programme and he expanded on those concerns the following month to the *Irish Examiner*.

My thoughts are with the young people. That's where it is. If they can associate a role model with something negative, be it alcohol, be it gambling, whatever, that's where I see the issue and I just prefer really if we could take it off the table.

It's not like the law isn't actually already there. There are amendments made there anyway. It's just whether they actually take a stand and whether they are willing to tackle such big companies or not. That's up to somebody else at a bigger desk. It's not like it couldn't be done as things currently stand . . .

The GAA are frontrunners when it comes to [prohibiting] alcohol branding. Credit where it's due, they're hugely out in front. They're PR-active and they're trying to do the right thing.

It's not part of our marketing. But it is heavily involved in other sports. As is gambling – two absolute poisons on society. No benefit has come to anybody from either of them.

I got a lot of slack from it online, as you always do. But the argument that came back was money. Revenue. I'm not a marketing expert but if there is a gap in the market because you get rid of alcohol branding, someone will fill it.

O'Hora wasn't the only Gaelic footballer to speak his mind in 2024. A tech summit was due to be held in Croke Park on 17 September that year, with Red Hat, a US software company owned by IBM, to host the event. It was postponed following strong criticism of Red Hat for its links to the Israeli Defence Forces, then engaged in savage attacks on the people of Gaza. Some of the most trenchant criticism came from prominent Dublin footballers, the likes of Jack McCaffrey, Philly McMahon, Michael Darragh MacAuley and David Hickey. When the postponement was announced, Hickey issued a brief statement: 'I am very happy and relieved that the GAA has stood up and let itself be counted on the side of Humanity, no matter the cost. So proud of Jarlath Burns and his colleagues. Thank you GAA. *Lux in Tenebris Lucet.*'

MacAuley stated: 'The GAA rightfully prides itself on its values. Showing solidarity with the Palestinian people is hugely important at the moment, and I am delighted that Croke Park have understood in this instance that some things are more important than money.'

In another context Shane O'Donnell, the 2024 Hurler of the Year, chimed in on the GAAGO controversy, which drove much of the Gaelic games discussion that season. The Clare man told the BBC's *The GAA Social* podcast (an unmissable listen among some very missable audio offerings):

The bottom line is I don't agree with [GAAGO]. Then I see on the GAAGO's website all year that they're selling the season pass with myself and three other players, just like right above the part where it says 'buy for X amount of euro'. To anyone, you could think that we're endorsing that or we have given our explicit consent that we would be put up there. And that's just not the case. We weren't even asked. I don't even want to benefit financially from that. I don't want to be endorsing GAAGO because I don't agree with it. So really, I just want them to ask me, can we put your image up there? [I'd say] no. It's not a huge deal, but you feel like you should have some control over your image. You want to be able to say, 'Yes, I'm happy to do that' or 'No, I'm not happy to do that.'

O'Donnell's calm explanation of his own position did a good deal of damage to the already stricken image of GAAGO. By dismissing the personal commercial implications in favour of a simple question of image rights he made a nonsense of any presentation of GAAGO as a community service. It was no surprise to see it folded into a new venture, GAA+, some months later.

While it might be an exaggeration to say that O'Donnell's argument was a nail in the GAAGO coffin, it – and the other cases mentioned above – may go some way to explaining another reason for managers shutting off players from the media. If more of them expressed their views and opinions on the major issues of the day, how influential would those contributions be on public opinion? Their managers might be unhappy at the possibility of their players being distracted, but for others in public life the prospect of GAA players swaying opinion could be a troubling one.

This is particularly interesting if GAA players don't take liberal positions. In the run-up to the marriage equality referendum of 2015 there were plenty of interventions from celebrities of all stripes, many of them advocating for a Yes vote. One of those who spoke out was Dublin All-Ireland winner Ger Brennan, who wrote in the *Irish Independent* that he would be opposing the 34th amendment, which would permit same-sex marriage.

I am voting 'No' because I don't want our Constitution to deny that it is a good thing for a child to have a mother and a father. The Universal Declaration on Human Rights proclaims that everybody is equal in dignity and it holds that marriage is a male–female union. I don't think the Declaration of Human Rights is homophobic. I'm voting 'No' . . . I know I'm not homophobic; my gay friends and family can attest to that.

The Dubliner could offer strong evidence to support his assertion that he is not bigoted. When he captained St Vincent's to the All-Ireland club football title in 2014 his acceptance speech thanked the girlfriends and boyfriends of the team for their support, and he was widely praised for his inclusivity. In follow-up interviews after that speech Brennan paid tribute to the likes of Dónal Óg and Conor Cusack for their openness about their sexuality ('The Cusack brothers, Dónal Óg and Conor, they would have stood up, they were true and honest with themselves').

Brennan's advocacy of a No vote might not seem to align with those views – in fact, assumptions might be made about his opinions on a range of subjects as a result. But it was notable that Conor Cusack acknowledged the sincerity of the Dublin man's beliefs in a radio interview. 'I think it's very healthy that people are allowed to express what's real for them,' Cusack told Today FM. 'And for me, a person who has an opinion like Ger's, he talks about being labelled homophobic or something like that. I would think, absolutely not.'

This kind of exchange on challenging issues is vanishingly rare among GAA players, who clearly have as many opinions on the topics of the day as anyone else.

It's not serving anyone to keep them muzzled while playing

to avoid controversies, and the surprise that players have opinions is the least of the drawbacks here. The viewpoints of public figures are of interest to the public, GAA players no more or less than any others.

HOW THE SPLIT SEASON IS NOT ONE OF THE GAA'S BELOVED ZERO-SUM GAMES

While I was talking to Shane O'Leary I brought up another challenge to GAA marketing: the split season. Compressing the inter-county season, ending with the All-Ireland finals in July, was a radical move but was embraced by the players themselves. Having concrete dates for fixtures allowed them to plan their year properly for holidays, for instance: a major win. But was it a victory when it came to selling the games?

'I've worked in sports marketing, and the biggest thing for any brand working with a sport is the opportunity to tell stories and to get stories out there. Generally that's with the fans but also, in an optimum world, obviously it's the players' stories. Allianz have done that really well, for instance. The key thing is getting your sport or your team into the public psyche through stories.

'As a child of the nineties I was brought up with the Sunday papers having a beautiful two-page story with a player or two, a hurler or a footballer, and the reporter would go for a pint or a cup of tea or whatever in the player's pub or living room. There was always something beautiful and juicy to come out of it; it wasn't the sort of sanitisation that you get now. You've had things like the Páidí Ó Sé documentary (*Marooned*), scenes with proper access, but that's all gone now. We actually have nothing.

'There's so much risk aversion and sanitisation in GAA, even compared to other, more professional sports, we now have none of that ability to tell the stories. For a country that sort of prides ourselves on like storytelling and association that's all about myths and old stories about Nickey Rackard and Christy Ring and so on – it's definitely hurtful that there's zero access to players and managers beyond, I would assume, sitting in front of them after the game. That's massively damaging from a marketing point of view. It doesn't allow you to tell the stories of the game and it limits the amount of mindshare or interaction or engagement you have with fans beyond the people who are the superfans.'

Hence the challenge of the split season. It's a concept with its supporters, and there are strong arguments in its favour. But it also has its drawbacks.

'There's a fairly ironclad rule of marketing generally that says the more your product is easy to remember and easy to buy, the more people that will buy it, the bigger it will be. That's fairly obvious. If you go into a shop on a hot day and you're thirsty, it's Coke or Coca-Cola you think of. It'll definitely be there for you because it's easy to get and you remember the red and white on the can. So make it easy to buy. The fancy terms are mental availability and physical availability. Is it mentally available and physically available?

'If you apply that premise and logic to the GAA, and particularly the season and the structure, we've made the window of opportunity to buy smaller because you've segmented the championship into a smaller amount of time. You've lessened your time on air as well. That goes back to the point made around the players not being available to the media. And you've sort of diluted the whole thing so you've lessened your mental availability, you've lessened then your physical availability. There's still the same amount of games available but it's in a shorter timeframe, and they don't get as much airtime on TV as well as space in the calendar. I just think it's a huge own goal, as has been said by many people smarter than me. It just does not make sense.

'I was a club player and I understand the club players as well, but the reality is the inter-county championship is the time when fans will get involved and if you want to maintain them then that's a major problem.'

It's compounded by being depicted as a zero-sum game. Either the season is as long as ever or it's months shorter; either players are flogged for months on end or there are no games at the height of the summer.

'This is the other thing. There's such knee-jerkism in the GAA, where it's "Right, we've tried this one thing, so now let's go to the exact opposite thing." There's a happy medium between where we are now and the length of time that we have and where we were before, which was maybe too long for the club games. But I definitely think there's a problem with the market-ability because of the length of the championship and also because of the amount of games.

'You're also impinging on the time of year when the other two big sports on the island are in their hottest moments. I was at the Champions Cup on the weekend that Wexford were playing Kilkenny in the Leinster championship. There were 30,000 people in London, some of whom might have attended that game or other games. And there was a lot of media focus and TV focus elsewhere compared to the space the Leinster Championship should have gotten on the weekend. And there was Gaelic football on that weekend as well.

'It just does not make sense to be trying to compete there when you have this golden timeframe and no other real competition in terms of bigger sports, and yet you've moved away from that. I just think it's a misstep, and I would assume they're looking to rectify it.'

The lack of access keeps the players mysterious, which may help with their aura when they're discussed on TikTok, but it militates against the popularity of the games. The argument could be made that players who aren't professional come to prominence from a variety of backgrounds and with different life experience, by contrast with professionals, most of whom come through a recognised career pathway. Yet GAA players, in all their infinite variety, remain largely unknown.

'If you look at other sports, and at rugby in particular, the guys that talk freely tend to be the people that are most sought after; they tend to tell the stories. I look at Mack Hansen, Ellis Genge – guys who have really interesting backgrounds, not your typical default sort of rugby story, and they're the ones that are sought after. They have the canvas to tell their stories. They can go on to podcasts, they can have pre-game chats, which GAA doesn't have. That's a big, big problem and you only get the sort of surface-level insight. You miss a Shane O'Donnell or Lee Chin or David Clifford – you don't get that level of behind-the-scenes knowledge with them. And that means that you don't know them as much. I know why it doesn't happen and I know coaches don't want to have the old "putting the piece of paper up on the dressing room of the opposing team, someone's said something wrong". The Canning issue is the one that's always pointed out.'

This was the famous Joe Canning interview after the drawn All-Ireland final in 2012. The Galway hurler's comments on Henry Shefflin in particular were widely publicised ('In one instance in the first half, Henry ran 30 or 40 yards down the field and was giving out to Barry Kelly and Damien Hayes for a free. That's not sportsmanlike').

Kilkenny won the replay and it is no exaggeration that over a decade later wary inter-county players were still citing the interview as a reason to steer clear of the press because Canning's comments had somehow, er, lost a hurling game. Sadly none of those players chose to remember the dozens of players who starred in and won All-Ireland finals after giving interviews. They didn't point out that in a healthy sports–media ecosystem, one unburdened by teams hiding behind amateurism, an interview such as Canning's wouldn't have stood out for its rarity, if nothing else.

But back to marketing, and Shane O'Leary spells it out in black and white:

'If we want to grow the game to keep it top of mind, and to do so in a more competitive scene, you need to bite the bullet. It can't just be when a player retires that they have the ability to tell that story; it has to be when they're playing.

'One of the things to look at for me would be mandated or regulated weekly press conferences during the championship season where you have access to two or three players and then possibly something like mandated access to one player for one paper every month. Something which is a bit more structured where media can get access to players in a more formalised way.

'Currently it's brands that get that access, the sponsors, but they're not going to tell a story that's in any way contentious. [They're] going to tell you that sort of positive, sanitised version, whereas a journalist has the ability to get stuff out of a person that they may not even want to say. It's too sanitised, and I think the GAA needs to put in mechanisms to overcome that and to regulate that a bit more. I think we underestimate the value still of the written word or the digital word or whatever getting that story out there.

'Yes, brands do a great job getting stories out but they'll come and go, and their emphasis is on telling the player story in a way that's relevant to whatever they're selling. For me, there's a little bit of an over-emphasis on using the brand as the story rather than using the media to tell the story, and the lack of press relations goes along with that.'

O'Leary also pointed out a real danger in GAA thinking on this matter: that banking on loyalty to the Association among consumers may be a fatal flaw.

'I totally agree it's a real missed opportunity and one of the points I made there around increasing competitiveness, there's a little bit of insular thinking in the GAA, an exceptionalism where they sort of go, "Well, we'll always be the priority."

'That isn't the case any more. People are way more willing to switch sports rather than necessarily be "born into the GAA family" than they were before. I think the GAA needs to maybe be more aware of that and not assume that they will always be the king of sports in the country.

'I'm not referring here to the "This is rugby country" non-sense here, but having said that, I was at the Rugby World Cup and the difference in the clientele from even ten years ago – I met a Mayo County Board member, lads from Wexford who'd never seen a rugby ball in their life . . . things are changing.

'The GAA needs to be mindful of that move and to facilitate players and managers getting their stories out there more effectively.'

BEING IN THE ROLE MODEL BUSINESS UNTIL YOU'RE NOT IN THAT BUSINESS ANY MORE

The choice was a simple one. In 2024 the Hurler of the Year shortlist was made up of three players: Shane O'Donnell of All-Ireland winners Clare; Darragh Fitzgibbon of All-Ireland finalists Cork; and Kyle Hayes of Limerick, who had been chasing a historic five All-Ireland titles in a row until losing to Cork at the semi-final stage.

O'Donnell, as a key man on the All-Ireland-winning side, was an obvious choice. Fitzgibbon had had a good season but a relatively average final. Hayes's year had ended before the final, the game that often doubles up as the coronation of the player of the year.

However, this became one of the more controversial selections not because anyone had a particular issue with O'Donnell's eventual victory but because of Hayes's backstory. Kyle Hayes was convicted of dangerous driving at Mallow District Court in September 2024. Judge Colm Roberts banned him from driving for two years and fined him €250 after finding him guilty of one count of dangerous driving on the N20 Cork–Limerick road, on 14 July. The previous March Hayes had been sentenced to two years in prison for violent disorder by Judge Dermot Sheehan. Hayes had pleaded not guilty to two violent disorder charges and one charge of assault, causing harm to Cillian McCarthy, in and outside the Icon nightclub in Limerick on 28 October 2019. He was convicted by a jury at Limerick Circuit Criminal Court in December 2023 of two counts of violent disorder and was found not guilty of assault. Judge Sheehan said it would be 'of no benefit to society' to give Hayes an immediate custodial sentence and suspended it. At the time of writing it was unclear whether that suspended sentence would be 'triggered' by the dangerous driving conviction: Hayes had appealed the latter but in March 2025 lost his appeal.

His status as an inter-county hurler was highlighted at one of the sentencing hearings when his manager with Limerick, John Kiely, gave a character reference on his behalf. Hayes went on to play a full role in Limerick's Munster and All-Ireland campaigns at half-back, but his presence on the shortlist for Hurler of the Year drew a good deal of flak. The court cases were fresh in the memory and there was plenty of criticism. Many observers voiced that criticism online, on the apparent basis that Hayes's crimes should have ruled him out of contention for a place on the Limerick side.

This seems a shaky stance, with some pretty obvious and familiar counter-arguments: that such awards are based on what happens on the field of play; that judging those awards has nothing to do with outside matters; and that if one were to start introducing complications such as removing someone from consideration because of legal difficulties, where would such exclusions end? Players are celebrated for their athletic prowess rather than their moral example, after all.

There is a powerful argument to be made, in fact, that sportspeople obsessed with victory and domination, who often have an unhealthy tunnel vision about their sporting goals and a disregard for social norms (to be generous), make for the *worst* role models not the best. The logic is obvious: because the vast majority of young people do not grow up to become savage competitors for whom defeat in any form is completely unsupportable – see more or less every high-achieving sports icon – following the example given by those icons makes no sense.

Becoming a well-adjusted adult is the achievable goal for most of us, an achievement that isn't something one would associate, for instance, with the Netflix documentary series *The Last Dance*, which revealed Michael Jordan's thought processes. Jordan's simmering on slights real and imagined helped to create the best basketball player of all time, though not perhaps someone most of us would like to sit next to on a long train journey. The late biologist (and baseball fan) Stephen Jay Gould perhaps put it best; he remarked that all one is owed by a sports star is sporting excellence, with anything in the way of moral example an unearned bonus.

The difficulty here, however, is not just that separating sportspeople from their sporting activities and off-field lives is more challenging than simply braying that sport is sport, and nothing which happens away from sport is relevant to that particular activity. It's more that Gaelic games stars are routinely held up for their moral example.

The man who won the 2024 Hurler of the Year award was celebrated in just those terms, in fact. Running in parallel with Shane O'Donnell's dazzling displays in the Clare jersey, with All-Ireland medals won eleven years apart, there's a significant academic career. He attended Harvard on a Fulbright Scholarship and has collected a PhD, while there have been suggestions he may be interested in becoming an astronaut in time. Little wonder that his alma mater, Ennis National School, paid this tribute to him in January 2023: 'Congratulations to past pupil Shane O'Donnell on receiving his well deserved Allstar last Friday night. Shane had an incredible year with the Clare hurlers and he is an unbelievable role model for our pupils to look up to. We are very proud of him here in ENS.' Or that his former teammate

Colin Ryan reached for this as a description when speaking to the press in June 2024: 'Shane is just a really impressive figure and certainly a great role model. He doesn't go looking for the limelight by any means but I suppose it's always going to come to a guy who's that good. He's a brilliant guy for kids to look up to. He does all the right things and he has a fierce amount of manners and respect to go along with it.'

Although an element of kennel blindness is understandable in those examples, the specific resonance of the inter-county star as role model is also a matter of particular importance to the players' representative body. Consult the Gaelic Players Association website and among the boilerplate commentary there's this: 'The GPA works closely with the Government at National and Local level through the Local Sports Partnerships by harnessing their status as role models and leaders in their communities to promote positive societal messages.'

In the first GPA AGM that accommodated in-person attendance after lockdown, chief executive Tom Parsons praised inter-county players as 'role models in their community, driving social change', adding in his address to the AGM that the organisation's members play 'a unique and irreplaceable role in Irish society, heritage and culture'. The GAA itself, in its learning resources for primary teachers, makes a similar point: 'Down through the years the GAA has given Irish boys and girls thousands of role models and heroes.'

Very well, the point is made over and over again. But difficulties arise when players do not measure up to those ideals. Hurlers and footballers have no exclusive hold on misbehaviour, of course. The Hayes case mentioned above ran in parallel, roughly, with another high-profile case, the conviction of former Irish rugby international Brendan Mullin for fraud. So did the conviction of former Irish soccer international Anthony

Stokes on drugs charges (and much thanks to the GAA person who was helpful enough to remind me of these). Were either of those instanced specifically as role models when in their pomp, though?

'I'm always a little bit wary of holding an athlete out as a role model apart from their sporting ability,' said Jack Anderson.

'In Australia there was an obvious comparison [when] Novak Djokovic wanted to play here during Covid but wasn't let into the country because he was anti-vaccination. The courts' general point at the time [was] that he was a role model and if he were allowed in then vaccination rates could potentially fall as a result. And I think most people would have felt at the time, "Would you really take health advice from some tennis player? Should you?"

'This is an area where you have to be careful. From my experience dealing with Australian sports bodies, for instance, what you're dealing with here is the fit and proper test to play a sport. If you're coaching a team at club or county level and a young fella comes to you and says, "Listen, I was at a party the other night and there's going to be an allegation made against me by a neighbour's child, I did nothing wrong, absolutely nothing, it's taken a huge toll on me but I'm absolutely innocent until proven guilty" . . . there's a big decision to be made there. If that goes to trial and some unpleasant facts emerge but he isn't found guilty, how do you deal with that? Those are big challenges. Even though the law may say someone is innocent, there are big moral and ethical questions here, and you've got to be very careful.

'So the minute you make a definitive statement – for instance, declaring the players are role models – you may be getting hoist on your own petard. You've got to be very careful with those things for a lot of reasons.'

Is part of the issue the sense that sport can be a refuge from the problems of the real world, which is understandable, but which can also lead to difficult discussions when the real world horns its way into sports discourse?

The real-world implications of a sportsperson's crimes are a good example.

'I completely get that. I remember dealing with an Australian sportsperson who had served time for an offence – not a sexual assault, something different – and then the issue was, when he came out, should you rehire him? Should any club take him on? Commercially it made complete sense, because he was a very good player, still young and able to contribute to a team, but from a sponsorship and spectator point of view they couldn't touch him, even though he had been rehabilitated and served his time.

'So I get that angle, that sport is a distraction and diversion but then real-world issues come in, and there's a need for people to really think about and reflect on those issues.

'Take the Rory Gallagher issue. When the GAA president intervened there it was inevitable the Kyle Hayes issue would be raised, with the accompanying question – Where is the policy here, what is the position? And the answer is that it's on a case-by-case basis, and that these are complicated matters.

'It's also worth pointing out that these are not professionals. They're not in an employment situation and this is technically a pastime. Even though they're members of the GAA, your oversight of them is not contractual: they're not employed, so that oversight is weaker, if you like. Clearly this shows how complex these issues are, and I would think will prompt a different response to similar issues in the future.'

Anderson's arguments were well made, as always, and the Rory Gallagher case mentioned illustrates the challenges here perfectly.

Gallagher stepped down as Derry manager in 2023 following allegations of abuse made by his estranged wife, Nicola Gallagher, allegations he denied. He was 'temporarily debarred' by the GAA in September 2023 while an independent panel investigated the claims made by his estranged wife. Gallagher successfully challenged that debarment in February 2024 and a statement from his solicitors in September said there was no 'legal impediment' to prevent him returning to a senior role in the game. 'I have engaged with every procedure available to me. The PPS [Public Prosecution Service] have issued two separate decisions finding that I have no case to answer,' said Gallagher.

However, when he was subsequently linked with a coaching role with the Naas club, GAA President Jarlath Burns rang the Kildare club to express his concerns, following up with an email in which he referred to decisions made by Naas that would 'reverberate far beyond your immediate community' and send a 'message about the values we uphold and the standards we set for our members and supporters'.

Naas then decided not to proceed with Gallagher's appointment, and Gallagher responded with a threat of legal action against Burns. In that response Gallagher stated: 'I await with interest to see if Mr Burns takes such direct personal action against others who find their private life the subject of social media commentary and hyperbole.'

When Burns appeared on *The Late Late Show* early in 2025 he addressed the Gallagher issue:

I hope he doesn't [take a legal case] but I can't retract anything I said in good faith in a private email to a club and I don't say that with any sense of ebullience or determination or, you know, 'bring it on'. This is a really tragic situation for a family. It shouldn't be getting discussed on *The Late Late*

Show . . . And there is always a way back for people. The GAA is not interested in cancel culture. There is always a way back for people and we have told Rory that as well. Rory is aware of the way back for him. I wish him and all of his family well and I hope we can reach a resolution on this.

Jack Anderson's point about dealing with issues on a case-by-case basis is worth reiterating. One size doesn't fit all.

But the GAA is on shaky ground when playing the role model card, on the reasonable grounds that not everyone who's a good hurler or footballer is necessarily a good role model. Readers may recall, in fact, that Jarlath Burns addressed this in the same episode of *The Late Late Show* in which he talked about the Gallagher case.

Kyle Hayes was convicted. Kyle Hayes is under the steward-ship of the Limerick management, [who] are outstanding people. Our players are role models, we expect a lot of them. But that is not what they sign up to. Our players are a reflection of the community and society from which they come.

Burns isolated the contradiction well: the players are role models but that's not what they sign up for. Still, withdrawing the role model label when it doesn't fit means it can't be applied with any seriousness at any time. Can the GAA really be in the role model business when that business is loaded with these contradictions?

THOSE WERE THE DAYS, EH? GAAGO

At the beginning of 2025 the GAA announced it was launching its own broadcasting service, GAA+. At the time of writing it was unclear how that would operate but surely safe to presume it would not draw the same storm of criticism that occurred the previous year over GAAGO, the joint operation between RTÉ and the GAA. This caused what we must by law describe as a firestorm of controversy because certain games were shown, and certain games weren't . . .

The best thing to do is to let one of the central characters talk. Which is why I asked Declan McBennett how much of the controversy was a general issue with RTÉ, which was in the firing line when the storm broke, and how much of it was the issue of GAAGO unto itself.

'I think you're right on both points. I think it needs to be looked at in cold, unemotional terms. And I think it did absolutely a hundred per cent get caught up in the RTÉ firestorm, and one thing led to another and the coincidence of timing around what was ultimately two matches.

'Number one was the Limerick–Clare game, which was nothing to do with GAAGO and nothing to do with us. Because it was moved. The Guards moved it. RTÉ already had it in its slot on the Sunday, but it was moved to the Saturday and it went to GAAGO. And then the second one was the Cork–Limerick game down in Páirc Uí Chaoimh, which was a brilliant night.

'So there was an awful lot of controversy around individual specific issues that tied into the RTÉ firestorm, that tied in turn into a political firestorm that became very, very populist.'

Before that GAAGO wasn't as prominent on most people's radar.

'I've always described GAAGO, until about five years ago, as a child. It took what it got and it fed the diaspora, and it performed no other function. What changed the landscape was Covid. Covid came along, and GAAGO grew from a child to an adolescent. It suddenly realised that it could do things that it couldn't do before, and it stepped into the breach in the middle of Covid when other broadcasters were asked to come to the table and didn't. The two broadcasters that stepped up were RTÉ and GAAGO.

'It also serviced the public. If you look at the history of it, the first iteration into it was WatchLOI for soccer. How that came about was two meetings involving myself, one with Niall Quinn, who was the acting CEO of the FAI [Football Association of Ireland] at the time. They needed to get the League of Ireland back or the clubs were in financial difficulty because they relied on bums on seats, and they were coming back before the GAA calendar. They needed to get their games out.

'GAAGO had no games to stream and was on the verge of laying people off. So two conversations happened, one with the FAI and one with GAAGO, and they both had the solution for each other. The FAI could provide games for GAAGO, which would stop the latter laying off people; GAAGO could provide an outlet for the FAI because the FAI didn't have the infrastructure to do it at the time. So WatchLOI was born, which then fed into the second half of this. That's Covid and the Covid championship.

'Games were brought to the people that they weren't allowed to attend. And as the GAAGO adolescent grew it became more ambitious as it moved into adulthood, and it said, "Right, what if we were to get these games as a rights holder and then show them?" With rights come responsibilities. So now you have to pay your bills as an adult. Once upon a time, there was a child taking what it was given, then the adolescent during Covid realised it could do a bit more, grew into adulthood, and that all fed into a narrative.'

McBennett stresses the changes brought about by Covid and particularly the realisation by many county boards that they could monetise games beyond simply charging those in attendance.

'Covid changed the world of streaming for GAA. Every county board is doing it and every county board bar one, I think, is charging money for it. And every county board wants to continue to do it. That causes issues around club coverage because counties want to ringfence their own. GAAGO did not invent the paywall or the streaming model for others. It was going to Sky previous to that. So the GAA crossed the Rubicon not with GAAGO but with Sky.

'If you look at it from an RTÉ perspective, there were three options. One was the GAA would do it on their own. Second, the GAA would do it with somebody else. The last choice was the GAA could do it with RTÉ, and RTÉ and the GAA already had a model to do it with: GAAGO. So from an RTÉ perspective, the natural thing was to say, "Okay, RTÉ and the GAA will do this together." The argument in principle and the ideological argument was around two things. First, should RTÉ be involved on a pay model basis, when your job, when your remit, is a public service broadcaster? And second, where is the money going?

'When the GAA gave the money to Sky, the money was going out of the country. When the GAA give the rights to GAAGO, the money went to three different locations. The money came in from the matches, and it either stayed in GAAGO to pay for the production, one; it went to the GAA in terms of both the rights and the dividend, two; and it went to RTÉ in terms of a dividend, three.

'So follow the RTÉ money. Where did the RTÉ money go? The RTÉ money came in and went straight back to the GAA in terms of paying for the league and the club. So there were more games on free to air as a result of games behind the paywall, because the licence fee was dropping, the commercial revenue was dropping. There was another stream to allow for greater coverage if the money was staying in Ireland. The money stayed in Ireland. The money went to the GAA. And when it went to RTÉ, it went back to the GAA. It didn't leave Ireland. The GAA will tell you that either eighty-four or eighty-seven per cent of their money goes back into the club, so the circle continued around that.'

McBennett's stress on the positives wrought by GAAGO are certainly worth considering, particularly as there was little appetite for hearing those arguments when the controversy caught fire.

'Ideologically, the paywall was not invented by GAAGO: it was there with Sky. But the fundamental difference around GAAGO was the money was staying in Ireland, more games were being done by GAAGO than were being done by any other outlet, and finally, more games were being done free to air by RTÉ as a result of having the money from GAAGO that allowed it to pay for the league and the club coverage.'

This last point was significant for RTÉ, certainly.

'Because one of the greatest criticisms of RTÉ, which was legitimate six years ago, was that RTÉ came to the table in May and left in September under the old championship model and wasn't seen for the rest of the year. RTÉ made a decision that it was going to have a calendar footprint across the GAA, and the calendar footprint now starts on the last weekend in January, when the league starts, and it continues into December when the club championships end, so now it has a calendar footprint across ten months of the year. It takes a break after the All-Ireland finals generally and doesn't do August and September, but it does October, November and December on the basis of club matches.'

Enter the politics in 2024. Did McBennett find the reaction of public representatives disappointing?

'No, I don't think it was disappointing. Because I think by the nature of what we do, we understand that we're going to get that level of criticism. I think it was frustrating, yes, for the simple reason that when it came before the Joint Oireachtas Committee the politicians really got involved. If you remember Micheál Martin – a genuine GAA person with his son playing for Cork and all that – took a view on this largely fuelled by the geographical basis of what was at play here.

'But other politicians who would be less GAA-inclined and less GAA-orientated suddenly saw that they could make hay out of this. There were individual concerns around Clare missing out on one particular year, Cork missing out on another particular year again, but those were quirks of the fixture list rather than any kind of deliberate decisions.

'When I went before the Joint Oireachtas Committee, ten minutes into that hearing I realised, somewhat naively, that the politicians weren't there to hear the answers. They were there to make political points with regard to soundbites for their local radio stations. That was particularly clear near your part of the world, because part of the criticism was around Kerry and the absence of David Clifford, in particular, from linear television on RTÉ rather than on GAAGO. So we went down through the number of games that Kerry had played and pointed out that nobody wants to see Kerry beating this team by 20 points and that team by 25 points.

'But the biggest frustration was when we had gone to the Kerry County Board the year before and asked them for one of their club semi-finals, featuring East Kerry and David Clifford. We were given the other club semi-final, which I think featured one single member of the Kerry panel, and the following day the Kerry County Board streamed East Kerry's game on their own streaming service. Yet RTÉ was ripe for criticism for not covering Kerry. So there was utter hypocrisy at play.

'The second part of the Oireachtas Committee was the grandstanding and parish pump politics going on with regard to "my county", or "me as a politician getting my clip on local radio in the morning, telling those boys up in Dublin what they should be doing and how they were betraying the people of Ireland".

'What they failed to recognise was that in 2018 RTÉ did forty live GAA matches. And from 2022, 2023 and 2024 they have done between seventy and eighty GAA matches. So the numbers virtually doubled. Camogie increased, club increased, league increased, Joe McDonagh [Cup] increased, Tailteann increased. Every single aspect of Saturday night highlights have come into play. Every single aspect of RTÉ's GAA coverage had increased, but the boys were happy to latch on to one match involving their county that didn't get shown without actually looking at the rationale behind it. So there you had parish pump politics at play, and it happened in all four provinces. If you go back and look at the politicians, the key individual politicians in that hearing came from each of the four corners of the country.

'The concept and rationale for GAAGO got caught in a political storm. To me what is forgotten about is Covid, when

GAAGO stepped up. Also, people should have followed the money, as I said: the money stayed in Ireland. And last, what were the consequences of GAAGO? Ultimately, the consequences of GAAGO were that more games were covered both by RTÉ and by GAAGO.'

Others were spared criticism at that time. Cork–Limerick was moved because of a concert in the Cork stadium, which few people picked up on. 'Correct,' said McBennett.

'I mentioned earlier on, there were two or three games that were at play. That Limerick–Clare game was moved by the Gardaí because there was a race in Limerick. Number two was the Cork–Limerick game, which was moved because of a concert. Number three was a Cork–Tipperary game which was a classic, one of the best, and everybody was giving out because that particular game was behind the paywall. But we did Cork–Tipperary the year before and Cork won by twenty points, and your own paper . . . described it as insipid and boring. As I've always said, if somebody can tell me what the classic matches are going to be next year, I'll happily pick them ahead of time.'

McBennett also forecast the coming of GAA+ during our conversation.

'With regard to the future, I think it is inevitable that ultimately the GAA will do their own thing, as every other rights holder has done, if you look at the NBA [National Basketball Association], the NFL, any organisation like that. But the reality of it is that the GAA was not equipped professionally, technologically, ideologically or otherwise to do what it did until the world changed – and a tiny percentage of that change in the world was Covid and the streaming of GAA.

'I don't think streaming is ever going away now, and I think more and more of it will be done by the GAA themselves.

Because what you have at the moment is you have this random nature of the GAA whereby a county controls coverage within a county, a province controls coverage within the province, the national competitions are at a different level, and individual fiefdoms are at play across the board. There needs to be a centralisation of that, as has happened with all other rights across the board, whether you look at UEFA [Union of European Football Associations] or FIFA [Fédération Internationale de Football Association] or the NBA or the NFL, or the AFL in Australia, eventually the same model would apply to Ireland.'

What about the 'being on both sides of the table' criticism that was raised at the time?

'I think that's a legitimate issue. I have always said, and I said at the Joint Oireachtas Committee, there was a sense of charges that were laid at GAAGO some of which stacked up and some of which didn't. So the conflict of interest was a recurring theme – the conflict of interest on the financial front was that RTÉ were benefiting from a paywall. To my mind, the issue [was] we were taking money, that we were involved in the production of, to generate more games. I understand the conflict of interest argument – I don't agree with it, but I understand the biggest issue with GAAGO, when you strip away the politics of it.'

Politics entered the argument elsewhere as well. McBennett makes a canny point about one of the challenges of the streaming service, which had little do to with RTÉ or the GAA and everything to do with infrastructural provision, which is of course the province of the same critical politicians.

'The biggest issue with GAAGO was an accessibility issue, not the payment issue, because the payment issue had been long since crossed. If you look at GAAGO, the value of the GAAGO compared to a county pass; there's one county in this country that charges €175 for its county pass.

'The biggest problem was accessibility. People want to sit down, hit one button on a television and be able to see the game. Here's what I would ask the politicians of the country, the very politicians who were giving out about the nature of GAAGO, the same politicians behind multiple broadband roll-out strategies across Ireland. If your broadband was good as mine was in south Armagh, you had no issue with GAAGO. Nobody ever complained about the production, the presentation or the games themselves. What they gave out about was, "I can't access it, it's the elderly people can't access it, it's buffering as I go" – all issues around accessibility. The same politicians who would happily stand over the roll-out of multiple national broadband policies didn't allow for that, so the GAA and RTÉ tried to overcome that by giving free passes to nursing homes and to GAA clubs.

'So instead of the famous man who lives down the by-road in the back end of Ballygobackwards not being able to see David Clifford on the television, the same man could go to his local GAA club and watch it there. He didn't have to go to the pub. If he went to his GAA club and watched there he could have his pint if he wanted or his water or 7-Up. He wasn't being driven to the pub.

'But in the same way that Covid changed the world with regards to streaming, the pace at which that happened was too fast for the GAA. They'd already sold these rights off to GAAGO and couldn't change that route. So they were on both sides of the table at the same time, but I don't think that will last for ever. In fact, I don't think it will last that long, and I think they will all be doing it in-house. The very principles of GAAGO will remain the same, and the issues of GAAGO will also remain the same: if your internet is good and you can access the games you're off and running. If your internet is poor, then GAAGO is a poor service, not because of GAAGO but because of your broadband and your internet.'

McBennett's prediction – made before the creation of GAA+ – came true. Perspective suggests both RTÉ Sport and the GAA were relatively unlucky to be collateral damage in the financial storm that engulfed the national broadcaster. However, the GAA certainly absorbed a key lesson from the summer of 2024 and ended up with its own streaming service.

PART 5
FACILITIES

PÁIRC UÍ CHAOIMH, OR AN END TO CORKNESS

Cork's showpiece stadium was intended to be just that – a jewel in the crown for the GAA, anchoring Gaelic games in the county with a dazzling tradition and hundreds of clubs. Instead, it became a cautionary tale.

All across the country, ambitious county board officers have Páirc Uí Chaoimh dangled in front of them as a warning. No matter how modest or grand their plans are – to upgrade a stand here, to redevelop dressing rooms there – they are given the example of Cork's stadium. An example to avoid at all costs, with costs being the operative word.

Yet for our purposes the stadium's various missteps and errors combine to make it an ideal case study, because the venue in Ballintemple is where so many of the GAA's challenges and interests come together. Sports and business. Fixtures and accessibility. Economics and values. Music. Hyper-local issues and the broadest contexts imaginable. Implications for society and for the GAA as a whole.

Refurbishing the Gaelic games facility on the banks of the Lee first became urgent over fifty years ago, when the old Cork Athletic Grounds was deemed no longer fit for purpose. It was duly replaced by Páirc Uí Chaoimh. This was seen as an impressive, modern stadium when it opened back in 1976, and the biggest club final attendance of all time was recorded that year when over 35,000 spectators saw Glen Rovers take on St Finbarr's in the Cork county hurling final.

Though players soon tired of the cramped dressing rooms, which urban legend held were based on a soccer stadium (11 players plus subs) rather than Gaelic games (15 players plus far more subs), it had its charms. The bowl effect of stands and terraces had the effect of sending spectator noise straight down onto the field, and (eventually) a fine playing surface hosted great days for every county in Munster, as well as Dublin in 1983's All-Ireland football semi-final replay.

However, as long-serving Cork County Board secretary Frank Murphy told the *Irish Examiner* some years ago, the debt on that refurbishment project became a problem almost immediately. The original estimate for the project was £1 million – sizeable in 1976 – but it soon ballooned to a total of £1.7 million. 'We paid very close on £900,000 on interest alone,' Murphy recalled. 'There was major concern about the possibility we were no longer viable.'

The board was in dire straits until it hit upon an innovative solution, enlisting Cork-born music promoter Oliver Barry to come up with the concept of Siamsa Cois Laoí as a way to pay off the debts. Along the way Barry more or less invented the modern Irish music festival, though that need not delay us unduly here. Suffice to say that Alan Stivell and Kris Kristofferson's turns in the Siamsa led to other even more profitable musical events in the eighties. Murphy added:

> The Michael Jackson concerts [1988] enabled us to buy Flower Lodge without bank borrowing. Those concerts made a huge difference, to be able to buy Flower Lodge without affecting the promotions of the games.

So a decade after starting the redevelopment, instead of facing bankruptcy, Cork GAA was able to buy another stadium, now called Páirc Uí Rinn, without going to the bank. Or without any affect on its core businesses, games promotion and development.

Now, decades later, another redevelopment. Another financial disaster. The upgrade of Páirc Uí Chaoimh was completed in 2017, but a massive overrun in costs has left the Cork County Board facing a €30 million bill. In a twist laden with irony, one of the consequences is a possible threat to Cork's great acquisition of the eighties, as the very future of Páirc Uí Rinn might be in danger. A large-scale transport plan for Cork, Bus Connects, might shear away part of the smaller stadium anyway: would selling the venue offer a way out of Cork's current financial mess?

Mess is not an understatement. When plans to redevelop Páirc Uí Chaoimh were mooted back in 2010 a total figure of €50 million to cover the costs of refurbishment circulated in news reports, though this seemed optimistic even then. The figure became €67 million by 2012 and that duly became €70 million in 2015, but by 2016 the cost was being estimated at €78 million. Two years later Croke Park's Peter McKenna told the *Examiner* he expected the cost would soar past €100 million. By September 2023, bank debt arising from the stadium redevelopment stood at €21,056,000. Annual loan repayments of €1.1 million were being made to service that total. Money owed by Cork County Board to Croke Park, meanwhile, stood at €7,763,722. The two figures combined reached almost €29 million, but county board officers acknowledged even then that legacy debt from the stadium redevelopment rested well above the €30 million mark. The December 2024 figures showed total debt standing at €31.1 million.

These are colossal figures for the GAA as a whole, and one county board in particular, to be dealing with. Even at the time of writing the specific reasons for the overrun remain a mystery, despite vague references to delays and bad weather and spiralling costs over the years, references which have never quite been worked up into a fully detailed explanation.

What is not mysterious is the stadium's disastrous history since reopening in 2017. Within two years of that reopening the playing surface had to be completely replaced, having torn up so badly the Cork County Board could not play games there until it 'no longer presents an injury risk to players'. The resurfacing works ended up costing €2 million. There were other challenges. In 2019 board officers told the annual convention that the board deficit was €560,000, but they were soon contradicted by the organisation's own audit and risk committee. The committee pointed out that figures from subsidiary companies, Páirc Uí Chaoimh CTR and Stáid Cois Laoí CTR, were not included in that figure. The true deficit was €2.4 million.

The audit and risk committee went further. Its members described the 'decision not to present the overall combined financial position to the convention' as a decision which 'questions the fundamental integrity of the Cork County Board'. They added that they would resign if it were not for 'the potential reputational damage to the Cork County Board' such an action would cause. All told, it was an extraordinary position for a financial oversight body to take.

More issues? In 2021, An Bord Pleanála ruled that Cork GAA should pay a special contribution of over €300,000 to Cork City Council; this was five times the amount initially offered by the board. In 2022 Cork County Board lodged a High Court suit against John Sisk & Son, the builders on the project, and Malachy Walsh & Co., the engineering consultancy that managed the redevelopment – two of the key operators who undertook the work. Another of those key operators was in the headlines in

2023: €4.4 million was the total paid by Cork GAA to settle a payment dispute with electrical contractor OCS, which was initially paid €7 million for its work on the rebuild before the court case was settled.

Even when the stadium was filled there were problems. For instance, the Munster–South Africa rugby game in Páirc Uí Chaoimh in November 2022 was viewed as a success on the basis that the venue was sold out. However, traffic chaos following the game marred the occasion for many of those in attendance, while John Cummins of the Cork City Fire Service said he was 'very, very concerned about the high-density packing towards the bottom of the Blackrock Terrace' at the game.

Mentioning that Munster rugby game recalls one of the key missed opportunities in the troubled history of the stadium: the Liam Miller charity game, when the GAA lost the chance to make Páirc Uí Chaoimh a destination stadium for the entire city. Cork native Miller, who played soccer for Celtic, Manchester United and the Republic of Ireland, died at the age of 36 in 2018. A charity benefit game was arranged for Turner's Cross that summer, but when Páirc Uí Chaoimh, with a far bigger capacity, was suggested as a better venue, the GAA said no. The consequence was a gigantic PR disaster for the GAA nationally, and for Cork in particular, with all concerned taking a fair beating in the court of public opinion. It was immediately pointed out, for instance, that €30 million in public money had been pumped into the stadium redevelopment, and government figures leaned heavily on the GAA to open Páirc Uí Chaoimh for the game. To its discredit, the GAA hid behind the rulebook, claiming its own rules forbade it opening the stadium to a charity soccer game – until the pressure became just too much and the stadium was made available anyway.

The obvious contrast is the alacrity with which the Munster–South Africa rugby game was embraced by the same organisation. The difference, of course, was that the rugby game was a commercial proposition, the kind of large-scale event which is a key component of the stadium's business, not a charity event. However, if the Liam Miller charity game had been embraced earlier and less grudgingly it would have surely helped to integrate the stadium into the life of the city. A more generous approach to that event would have framed the venue as a key attraction and welcoming space, not a distant, forbidding monolith at the back of a public park.

Siamsa Cois Laoí fulfilled that role back in the seventies, drawing a different audience to the stadium when it was newly opened. Whether those grooving to Don McClean and the Wolfe Tones ever returned to watch intermediate hurling games is not the point: the concerts helped to make the stadium a part of the city. This was clearly one of the aims when the new stadium was envisaged – to make it a central part of life on Leeside. In the various iterations of the redevelopment plan a GAA museum and coffee shop appeared in the proposals. They remain sketches on planning documents, while other potential improvements have also been ignored.

When Peter McKenna of Croke Park sounded the alarm about the vast mounting debt in 2019, he also pointed to easy wins for the stadium management: 'We need to lift the branding. We have to make it feel red on every staircase, every corridor, every meeting-room. Team photographs, team colours. You have to know you're in the heart of Cork GAA when you're there.'

Opportunities to showcase the venue have been missed since then. When Cork reached the All-Ireland senior hurling final in 2021 the stadium didn't reflect that achievement during the build-up, when the county colours would have been expected to figure prominently. Then again, it was also almost impossible for the Cork hurlers to get even an hour's training done in the stadium before that final.

This raises another spectre running in parallel with the various building and infrastructural issues: the impact of the stadium on Cork's games development and promotion. The cost overruns in Páirc Uí Chaoimh have had an impact on the games side, despite Cork officials insisting over the years that tackling the debt would not have a negative impact on how inter-county teams are run. In 2022 Ed Sheeran concerts were hosted in the venue, concerts that were obviously necessary to pay off some of the stadium debt. But this meant preparing the stadium for a concert and then restoring it to its original purpose afterwards. That meant closing the stadium to sports, which in turn meant the Cork senior teams had to move. The footballers, facing Kerry, and the hurlers, taking on Clare, lost home advantage for vital championship games; Cork officials said at that time that they would ensure that future concerts would not be in conflict with championship games, but that soon changed. In 2023 Cork GAA CEO Kevin O'Donovan told a county board meeting: 'It is not viable to rule out concerts in any particular time of the year, but again, with minimum effect on our teams.' In 2024 remedial work to the Páirc Uí Chaoimh surface in the aftermath of a Bruce Springsteen concert meant the venue was off limits when Ulster champions Donegal visited in June.

Also, while soccer and rugby have brought large crowds to the stadium, blue-chip GAA games have not been as plentiful as might have been expected. Cork GAA officials were disappointed not to get the 2023 Munster hurling final, for instance, which would have been both a showcase for the venue and a major boost for local businesses. But with officials in other counties warned repeatedly not to match Cork's profligacy when it comes to their own projects, sympathy for the Rebels – and the problems it had created for itself – was in short supply. At provincial level Cork certainly didn't appear to wield the power it had in past decades when it came to significant decisions, such as hosting Munster finals.

It also took seven years for Cork to come up with a main sponsor for its ground – not surprising given the slew of controversies surrounding the stadium – but that's not to say Cork GAA wasn't trying to raise money beyond stadium sponsorship. In 2020 it launched a 'Rebels' Bounty' draw, with different sales targets for clubs according to their grades – senior clubs in the county were required to sell 100 tickets, intermediate clubs 70 tickets, junior A clubs 55 tickets and junior B clubs 35 tickets. With tickets costing €100 each club would retain revenue on tickets sold beyond these base numbers, but they were supposed to be liable for any shortfall if those targets were not met. If a junior B club was left with ten unsold tickets, for instance, it would have to pay €1,000 to the county board for them. The following year, however, it emerged that some clubs had successfully negotiated lower sales targets for themselves, depending on their circumstances, though others were meeting and exceeding their original targets. The nature of the scheme had drawn some criticism from smaller clubs, which pointed out that sparsely populated areas and low membership would make sales challenging.

That grumbling was as nothing, however, to the criticism drawn by the national shambles that was the SuperValu deal. In January 2024 the *Irish Examiner* broke the story that SuperValu was to come on board as Páirc Uí Chaoimh's sponsor, with one crucial part of the story catching everyone's eye: Cork's stadium would be rebranded accordingly as SuperValu Páirc or Park. What looked like an ideal commercial partnership with

SuperValu, a Cork company with a genuine track record of community involvement all over the country, immediately became a disaster. Then Tánaiste Micheál Martin was quick out of the blocks, articulating his disappointment with the name change on X: 'Deeply disappointed & annoyed at the proposal to change the name of Páirc Uí Chaoimh. Pádraig Uí Chaoimh was a key figure in the formation of the GAA at club and national level. Govt allocated €30m towards the development of the stadium and never sought naming rights.'

As a member of the same club as Pádraig Ó Chaoimh, after whom the stadium was named, Martin's annoyance was understandable. His brother Seán, a Nemo officer and city councillor, went a good deal further:

You are sacrificing our tradition, our heritage, and our history. We need to hang onto our historical figures who built the organisation. He's [Ó Chaoimh] definitely one key person in building the organisation, both locally and nationally.

In this modern world, we often have change for the sake of change. There are some things you hang onto, this is one of them. Within Nemo, there is strong respect for history and tradition and what he gave us. There is disappointment at this decision.

There is a need for us not to forget where we came from and why there was a need for the GAA. This goes against that.

Regarding the deal itself, Seán Martin added:

There is an issue there with the Páirc Uí Chaoimh debt. This deal is not going to destroy the debt or put a big hole in the debt. I suspect it will help towards Cork's expenses for the year. The €30 million debt is a bigger issue altogether.

They need to come up with a proper programme of investment and how they are going to get the money to pay off the debt going forward.

The deal was in the headlines and debated on the airwaves for days, with Cork GAA officials lambasted; when the Ó Caoimh family pointed out that they had not been consulted on the name change it proved a telling blow, and eventually the backlash was too strong to resist. The name of the stadium would be SuperValu Páirc Uí Chaoimh. In one last hilarious effort to snatch a draw from the jaws of defeat, Cork officials tried to paint the ferocious criticism which greeted their plans as somehow showing the strength of their brand.

The size of Cork's stadium overrun means investment in a full centre of excellence is out of the question, something that has implications down the line for the development of players and for competitiveness on the field of play. Yet at the end of 2024 Cork GAA suggested that the development of a centre of excellence is a key objective over the next five years, circulating a strategic plan with repeated reference across the 41-page document to a new 'home for our teams'. How this would be paid for when the board is on the hook for over €31 million is not clear (the hidden costs of 'centres of excellence' is dealt with elsewhere in this book), but a general lack of clarity in Cork is no shock.

Cork GAA banned media representatives from its monthly meetings early in 2024, leading to some surprise when one official blamed inaccurate reporting of measures introduced by the board the following year. The measures referred to were levies introduced by the board to help with the stadium debt, even though in the past officials such as former chairperson Tracey Kennedy had taken another view. She said in 2019:

It is our intention not to impose levies on clubs but there is no denying the fact that pressure will come on us in terms of meeting our commitments, and we have to ask our clubs to help us with a club ticket model, which is planned for the stadium. Our clubs and all our supporters need to be part of our journey but I don't see that by imposing levies.

This was echoed by Cork GAA CEO Kevin O'Donovan the same year:

We can talk for ever about levies or not [imposing] levies. We would hope that there would never be a levy placed on clubs to fund bricks and mortar but at the same time we have to face the harsh reality that it's our stadium.

Six years later those levies were announced anyway.
The journey continues in Cork, but the ramifications go far beyond its borders.

* * *

It would be wrong to say that Páirc Uí Chaoimh provides a neat picture of the challenges facing the GAA as a whole. Nothing about the stadium in Cork is neat. But it does provide a central narrative that draws in many of the challenges facing the Association as a whole, from top to bottom. For instance, when does Croke Park step in and take over a situation the local officers can't handle?

There have been situations in the past where Croke Park has had to send an outsider into a county to restore order. In 2012 long-time Munster GAA official Simon Moroney was sent by GAA Director General Páraic Duffy to advise the Kildare County

Board on its finances following an advance of funds from Croke Park to help the Leinster county avoid financial difficulties. That advance amounted to approximately €300,000 or one-hundredth of Cork GAA's debt on Páirc Uí Chaoimh.

Croke Park has already been in charge of the Cork stadium. It took over Páirc Uí Chaoimh in 2018, but by 2020 Cork officials stated that they were back in command. The situation has not improved since, with the debt remaining north of €31 million. It could be argued that Croke Park should simply take charge of the stadium again. If that were to happen other counties would become restive, as such a move would create a precedent for losing control of their own venues and premises to Croke Park if difficulties arose. As one officer confided to this writer, what would the threshold of difficulty be in his county? Nowhere else might generate an overrun of €30 million, as in Cork, but a smaller county might soon find it had lost its independence for far smaller amounts.

Another key takeaway from the Páirc Uí Chaoimh mess is the importance of the GAA maintaining good relationships with government, whether that is at national, local or permanent level. Micheál Martin was Tánaiste when the SuperValu controversy erupted and was Taoiseach at the time of writing. As a dyed-in-the-wool GAA person he should be a huge asset to Cork GAA and Croke Park alike, but his anger with the proposal to drop his clubmate's name from the stadium in Cork was deep and genuine. It can't be good when the most powerful politician in the country is publicly reminding a sports organisation of the conditions attached to exchequer funding it received. (Or, as Martin stressed pointedly, conditions about naming rights it *didn't* attach.)

At a local level Cork GAA's contentious relationship with the local authority had to be settled eventually by An Bord

Pleanála, which ordered Cork GAA to pay a special contribution of over €300,000 to Cork City Council in relation to the expansion of Páirc Uí Chaoimh, five times the amount the sports body believes was the appropriate sum. That was in 2021, the same year Cork City Council turned down an application from Cork GAA to increase car parking around the stadium. Good working arrangements between local GAA authorities and municipal bodies are mutually beneficial; in an extreme example, during Storm Éowyn Kerry County Council designated local GAA clubs as community hubs for people left without power and water. Large-scale organisations such as local authorities and sports bodies with a presence in every parish need to be able to work together. The fact that Cork's relationship with its city council needed the arbitration of an organisation with the reputation of An Bord Pleanála is yet another an example other counties would want to avoid.

Relationships are little better with the permanent government. As far back as 2015 there were media reports that an initial payment of €10 million from public funds towards the redevelopment costs of Páirc Uí Chaoimh had been held back following concerns expressed by the Department of Public Expenditure and Reform. Reports claimed specifically that worries over the board's cost–benefit analysis report, and projected attendances for non-sporting events in particular, were the main reason for the funds being withheld. In a statement at the time the Cork County Board denied that any money had been withheld and insisted that they were 'fully engaged' with the Department and that talks were ongoing.

The warning for other counties from this episode is twofold. The first is to have a bulletproof cost–benefit analysis done ahead of large projects. The concerns expressed in 2015 found an echo ten years later in comments from Cork GAA CEO

Kevin O'Donovan: 'Concerts in this building [Páirc Uí Chaoimh] are challenging because we're a mid-size venue. We're too big for Live at the Marquee, we're too small for Coldplay. We talk to the promoters every day, we are seeing now if we can move the dial a little bit and go into smaller events and use car parks and use 4G and put marquees up on the pitch and so on.' The second lesson is a simpler one: don't have delays in funding, as they can multiply costs disastrously.

Bringing the public with you is another key lesson from Cork's experience with Páirc Uí Chaoimh. The SuperValu fiasco and the PR disaster of the Liam Miller charity game are not the only blots on the Cork copybook. Yet another fundraising scheme came a cropper in July 2020, when the Cork County Board abandoned a controversial plan to charge All-Ireland medal winners for their match passes to games within the county, a plan that had been widely criticised when mooted at a previous board meeting. For one hundred years Cork players who had won an All-Ireland senior medal in football or hurling had traditionally been entitled to a pass allowing free admission to games in the county for life, and the Board was forced into an embarrassing climbdown when there was a negative reaction to the plan.

The following year it emerged that the Cork Camogie Board had been billed for using the stadium. The Cork senior camogie side that contested that year's All-Ireland final was charged €500 for playing a challenge game in Páirc Uí Chaoimh that August, and stadium representatives said that the Cork County Board would be charged by the stadium authorities for senior club championship games in the stadium as well as for challenge games played there by the county teams. The need to generate revenue is obviously a pressing one, but are occasional sums of €500 worth the effort? The negative publicity involved almost outweighs the entry in the balance sheet, but the proposed removal of All-Ireland winners' match passes leaves no room for ambiguity. Not only was it an appalling way to treat players who had given years of service, it had the simultaneous effect of alienating a cohort of high-profile players who would be the ideal people to market any schemes aimed at raising funds to offset the stadium debt.

* * *

The last issue raised by the SuperValu controversy is a slightly more existential one. It's Marketing 101 for any organisation to seek association with another body or organisation more closely identified with various social virtues. The whole reason financial organisations look to sponsor or endorse sports teams or competitions is to reflect in the glow of athletic virtue. How can you think of us as rapacious capitalists, after all, when our name is on your kid's top?

The GAA is no different; it attracts sponsors of all kinds and sizes who want to be seen as benevolent and benign. No shock there. The GAA's core values of voluntary effort and community involvement are powerful and powerfully attractive to businesses. In that sense, what could be more GAA-coded than using the name of an obscure administrator for a twenty-first-century stadium?

However, the suggestion that the name Páirc Uí Chaoimh might be dropped for a company's name marked a turning point and not in a good way. If that possibility was on the table it meant that everything was on the table. If money could displace a name in that way it suggested that the GAA was moving away from its core values. Second, such a move drastically reduces the GAA's attractiveness to those large-scale sponsors. If the values mentioned above are not obvious and visible, what is the benefit of association for such companies? Third, and most dangerous, such a move would mean the GAA no longer emphasises those values.

There's something extraordinarily short-sighted in even mulling over the possibility of removing the name of Páirc Uí Chaoimh. If the basic attraction of the GAA is its standing in society – the voluntarism, the universal welcome, the community, 'where we all belong' – anything that contradicts those values has the potential to derail that standing.

If the GAA is willing to sell the name of its second-biggest stadium, what else is for sale? Even more dangerous for the GAA: if it's willing to sell anything it's no different from any other organisation.

That would be a far bigger threat to the GAA than any debt.

BUILD IT AND THEY WILL COME

The edifice complex is strong in the GAA. Bricks and mortar venues have never really lost their appeal. Yet there is also a general recognition that there are too many GAA stadiums around the country. Often venues are too big for the constituency they're supposed to be serving, or there are two of similar size in the one county where – whisper it – only one is really needed.

Why does the GAA need another half-billion euro for premises, then?

In October 2024 GAA President Jarlath Burns told RTÉ:

> Looking around the country we are doing a lot of stadium rebuilding and refurbishment. What was acceptable twenty or thirty years ago in terms of spectator comfort is no longer acceptable. You go to watch a game and everything from 'eating to excreting' has to be as good as a hotel. We don't come up to scratch a lot of the times on that in the GAA.

Burns had already touched on the GAA's infrastructure challenges in a previous interview that year with the national broadcaster:

> In the next two years, we are becoming a fully integrated organisation. As a result of that, Cork, Armagh, Down, Longford, Carlow, Kerry, Monaghan and maybe four or five other counties are upgrading or building centres of excellence

and making them facility-correct. Each one of those is going to cost about €15 million to build. That's about €200 million we have to find in the next three years. Kildare, Louth, Meath, Waterford, Antrim, Kerry, and Thurles are upgrading their stadiums. That's another €200 million. So I would say in the next three or four years, give or take, we have to spend half a billion on infrastructure.

The stadium dilemma was recognised by others, including Jack Anderson.

The GAA really needs to look at its capital investment programme. The AFL basically uses six stadiums to run its season and it only owns one stadium. The GAA owns lots of property but building, maintaining, refurbishing, etcetera multiple 30,000-seater stadiums is no longer necessary. There is a bit of the 'tulip bubble' about it all. Smaller stadiums with better facilities and built as community hubs is much better.

In his comments to Congress in 2024 Tom Ryan sounded a similar note:

We need to approach GAA capital projects differently. Shared development have long been anathema to our thinking, I know, but if we can share with universities, share with other organisations then why not share between ourselves? What would our infrastructure landscape look like if we were to prioritise half a dozen facilities around the country for prioritised investment, remove the local funding burden, and designate them as provincially or nationally shared? Don't dismiss it out of hand.

Fair enough. But what about the ones the GAA already has? They can't be sold for apartments. Or can they? Nickey Brennan, former GAA President, said:

'That might not be as daft as you think. Because if you look at some of the stadiums in England, they have incorporated some class of accommodation as part of the venue's commercial activity, like a hotel. So absolutely, I think that that should be explored in a number of cases.

'Yes, we have too many stadiums, but you're not going to get rid of them. Whatever about downsizing – and when I say downsizing I mean can you actually develop the site to be used for something else and maybe generate some sort of an income stream? The GAA are not going to do that. You'd have to get some commercial partner on board. Yes, the GAA has understandably developed commercially around the Croke Park Hotel and the next hotel that's going down into Clonliffe College. There's logic in that, because it will deliver a consistent revenue stream to the Association. There's a commercial reality there.'

There's also a behavioural reality. The odd outlier apart – Cork–Limerick in the Munster championship in 2024, for instance – attendances are not at the same level.

'If you're recognising that the income from games is going to reduce, you therefore want to look at revenue streams like hotels, concerts. And we can argue that yes, concerts now are taking over some of the good parts of the summer of games, and that's a valid argument as well.

'But there is also a challenge for stadiums right now. Let's take the likes of Thurles, Killarney, Limerick – the reality is because of the size of those stadiums, maintenance is a significant factor. Because the steel in the building and various other parts of the venue deteriorates, the ongoing money needed to maintain them is very significant for the amount of games that they get, particularly the types of game that test their capacity. So it's a poor economic return. But what do you do? You can't talk to those three stadiums and say, you have to close this one or that one down.

'I do think it's going to mean a fair bit of thinking outside the box: can some commercial partners be brought in that maybe could develop some commercial enterprise there? The notion that those stadiums continue as they are and continue having to be maintained is going to draw a fair bit of finance over the coming years, and that's going to put pressure in turn on county boards, provincial councils and, indeed, Croke Park.'

There's also a hierarchy of needs among those stadiums, Brennan pointed out.

'You have Casement Park, which is slightly different, but you have Louth, Kildare, Waterford (which is being done), Navan. They need work simply to make them more accessible to people. Jarlath [Burns] was quoted as saying half a billion is needed for infrastructure, which is completely beyond the capacity of the GAA.

'Having said that, when we built Croke Park we borrowed something like two hundred million, which made a lot of people very nervous. But within a very short period that was well in control. I think people were astounded then, but we're living in very different economic times now. Don't forget either that the GAA would be investing about half a billion in infrastructure which would not be able to turn the kind of profit that Croke Park could within a few years.'

Peter McKenna, Croke Park's stadium and commercial director, the man who enabled Croke Park to turn that profit, also sounded a note of caution.

'We have to be careful not to over-index on building. The requirements of health and safety, people's reasonable expectations of a stadium experience are becoming higher; the costs associated with meeting those demands are getting higher and higher. So are upkeep and maintenance. Sometimes those costs aren't considered. At club level they tend to be small, and a local tradesman, who may be a member of the club concerned in any event, can look after repairs and maintenance.

'But obviously, you bring those costs to a two hundred- or three hundred-million euro facility and they escalate. There are lights, LEDs, heat, safety requirements, and it starts to become massively expensive. We would put aside five to six million every year just to keep the premises [Croke Park] as is – not to upgrade, just to keep it as it is. Painting walls, tidying up bits and pieces; maintenance can sometimes be overlooked a little when planning around facilities.'

Is it unrealistic to expect a Croke Park-level experience at other grounds around the country?

'I think it's even more basic than that. It's not that we're "posh", but just that basic standards can be missing. Take the quality of bathrooms, women's facilities, good-quality food – all of those things need to be focused on, and frankly some facilities are just not good enough. Women don't want to go to games in those facilities because the bathrooms there are grim, full stop. We would do well to see [them] hitting minimum standards. If someone comes to the facility in a wheelchair, are they able to get to the viewing platform in comfort? Do they have to go over cobbled stones or rough ground to get into the venue? Are the women's facilities being cleaned properly and regularly?

'Now, people are going to the venue to watch a match at the end of the day. They're not going for a romantic meal. Even in Croke Park food is part of the add-on, the service provision, not the main event, but people are still coming from Cork and Donegal and all parts of the country with reasonable expectations about the basic levels of those add-ons.

'In this area it's all very well to think about shooting for the stars, but sometimes I think we need to have a closer look at the launchpad.'

In Kerry's case the launchpad has already proved challenging, and it may in time prove a test case for prioritising facilities. In November 2024 Kerry GAA recorded an operating profit of €506,262 for 2024 and a retained profit of €787,888, which suggests a well-run organisation. But is it well-run enough to sustain a redevelopment project of €77 million? The *Examiner* reported late in 2024 that Kerry GAA had an ambitious €77 million plan for Fitzgerald Stadium, 'which they intend to transform into a sports, tourism and entertainment attraction. They have commenced a legal process to draw down monies from the Immigrant Investment Programme, which has now closed.'

First, Kerry officials needed to look east to see the example of Páirc Uí Chaoimh, the perfect illustration of how costs can rise, though it should be pointed out that in 2022 the cost of redeveloping Fitzgerald Stadium was estimated as approximately €72 million; within 12 months it had risen to €77 million without any work taking place. Some concern had already been expressed locally about the size of such an investment for a stadium filled perhaps once a year for a Munster football final not to mention the telling inclusion of an 'entertainment' component to the complex. If Killarney looks east (again) they might see that entertainment may not be quite the money-spinner it expects. There's a clear cautionary tale in Páirc Uí Chaoimh being neither big enough for the headliners nor small enough for up-and-coming acts. Would Fitzgerald Stadium, even a new and improved version, fall into the same trap?

It was also interesting that when Kerry GAA was allocated €6 million by the government in late 2024, Dingle GAA club piped up with its disappointment that it had not received any funds in that year's allocation. While the west Kerry club was careful to wish Fitzgerald Stadium well, it also pointed out in a statement that it and other small organisations would be in competition with the stadium for funding – a somewhat daunting proposition.

Would it be more feasible for the GAA, and for the GAA in Kerry, to sell the site for housing and take the resulting windfall to reinvest in Austin Stack Park in Tralee, the biggest town in the county and often the venue for county games in any case? In that scenario the default venue for the biggest Gaelic football games in the province might have to be Páirc Uí Chaoimh. That might be unthinkable in the Kingdom, but similar arrangements have been suggested in other counties, as we shall see.

Further north, Tipperary GAA had a different challenge on hand. The *Examiner* reported in September 2024: 'Semple Stadium requires a €4 million investment from the GAA to maintain the upkeep of the fabled venue and there remain hopes to revive the pre-pandemic redevelopment plans they had for the Kinane Stand, which at the time were estimated to cost €10 million.' Tipperary were deeply disappointed, then, to lose out when Large Scale Sports Infrastructure Funding (LSSIF) of €137 million was announced in November 2024. Fitzgerald Stadium's west terrace in Killarney received €6 million in those allocations, Clare GAA's centre of excellence in Caherlohan €3.2 million and €650,000 went to pitch facilities in Patrickswell GAA club in Limerick, but Tipp were left with 'great disappointment and utter devastation', according to the county chairman. There can be some internal tension in counties when one project benefits over another, but there can also be a little envy between counties when one showpiece stadium is funded and another isn't.

Meanwhile, in the south-east the stadium challenge is obvious. Irial Mac Murchú lives a 15-minute drive from Fraher Field in Dungarvan. It's another 40 minutes onwards to get to Walsh Park, so it's no surprise that he's clearly fonder of the nearer venue.

'Dan Fraher bought that field, some of the early All-Irelands were played there. There's a history there, and we all own that history. He was a fluent advocate for the language as well as Gaelic games, and we all have an emotional, historical and social investment in it. There's a value to that; that was where our county finals were played.

'There is the argument as well that the GAA needs a lot of money to survive. Yeah, I love being in the GAA but the one thing I hate about being in the GAA is having to sell tickets. I'd nearly buy the tickets myself.

'I was on a national committee a few years ago when I was nominated by Aoghán Ó Fearghail to a policy review committee and got an insight into stadiums and their capacities and their need and all of that kind of thing.

'We're obsessed in the GAA with stadiums – we don't need as many big stadiums. We have in Munster alone Páirc Uí Chaoimh, Thurles and Páirc na nGael, three fine big grounds. Add to that Ennis, Dungarvan, Tralee and Killarney.'

And yet and yet and yet. Mac Murchu gives a good explanation of the appeal of a home venue.

'I was in Walsh Park for Waterford's most recent championship games. We might get a hell of a lot more people if the game was held in Thurles but those games in Walsh Park, the days the hair stood up on the back of your neck.

'When Timmy O'Keefe was secretary in Waterford some years ago he made a proposal which people thought was outlandish at the time – that Waterford would play their home games in Nowlan Park in Kilkenny and forget about spending millions on Walsh Park. He was lambasted in certain quarters but he did have a point. Not that I would be happy to be driving to Kilkenny for Waterford games, but in economic terms, the cost of running the GAA, the cost of running the stadium, the cost of developing the stadium, where do you stop?

'Apart from the very biggest inter-county games, attendances are in decline. I remember in the eighties when my own club here, An Rinn, were playing senior football against clubs like Ballinacourty and Stradbally and you couldn't fit another person into Fraher Field. That was before health and safety. That was when all the banks were full. But I was at a senior football game recently, and I don't think there were five hundred people there, yeah. Bigger stages, smaller crowds, it doesn't add up.'

In the end Mac Murchú tied the two issues together: the need for fewer stadiums; and the equally strong need people express for their own venues.

'I think that there is a very strong case to be made for maybe up to seven or eight regional stadiums in the whole country. Casement Park is badly needed for Ulster, for the second biggest city in the island and for the huge resurgence up there. But where do you draw the line? What's big enough, and what's too small? So Fraher Field – it's a county ground but I don't think it's ever plausible that anyone would ever suggest selling it. I think that a consortium of people would almost get together and buy it between them, such is the emotional association within the GAA, and that's part of what we are.'

THE SECRET HIDDEN IN THE CENTRE OF EXCELLENCE

In a conversation many years ago with an inter-county manager I asked, in my naivety, why one of his selectors was . . . how to put this nicely? . . . a bit of an ignoramus. Most of an ignoramus, actually. Others in the backroom had obvious functions that related to their various strengths: defence coach, attack mastermind, amateur psychologist, vibes merchant, and so on. The roles might not have been that sharply defined, but the division of labour was pretty clear. But this other buck?

It was easy, said the manager. There was no shortage of people who fancied being a selector if it meant standing on the sideline during a game and pointing out switches and moves that should be made. But, he added, there was a terrible shortage of people who could organise, say, a pitch for training at two hours' notice. If a club rang the manager and said their field was suddenly unavailable, he could pick up the phone to this particular selector, who would source a venue within an hour. Invaluable. The toes he trampled on in doing so was not the manager's concern, he added.

Then he said, 'Of course, if we had our own place to train . . .' Contrary to what you might imagine, not every county has a dedicated space for its county team. Or for all its county teams. A space with a gym and meeting rooms and a working kitchen and dressing rooms near a playing field, or more than one playing field. Hence the newest obsession of every county board: the centre of excellence.

Most of them would love to be in a Tyrone-type situation. In December 2023 Tyrone GAA had fully cleared all the borrowings – some £2.5 million/€2.9 million – on its Garvaghey Centre of Excellence facility. The borrowings were all from Croke Park and were cleared to plan. The Garvaghey site and its facilities cost £8 million sterling/€9. 3 million: over 60 per cent of that was raised within Tyrone GAA, helped by its official supporters' wing Club Tyrone. Croke Park contributed 20 per cent funding, and the EU's LEADER Rural Development Programme funded 11 per cent. The Northern Ireland Assembly put in just under 10 per cent. All in all, a tidy job.

And in stark contrast with Cork GAA, which in December 2024, despite its €31.1 million debt and a serious delay in its plans to cash in on land it had earmarked for a lucrative development on the northside of the city, stated that the development of a centre of excellence was a key objective over the next five years. The Cork GAA Strategic Plan 2025–30 contained repeated references to a new 'home for our teams', stating that 'the lack of training facilities threatens to undermine the incredible work done by both voluntary and professional personnel with our county teams', while all inter-county managers 'are united in the belief that the requirement of a home for our teams is now essential'.

One significant point needs to be made about high-performance facilities, one which isn't often made when counties are considering centres of excellence. They cost money but don't earn money unless the game is professional. A soccer club that brings a player to prominence through its high-performance facility will benefit financially, obviously, if the player's sold to another club. A rugby club with elite performance facilities may benefit through a successful, well-prepared team and be rewarded financially accordingly as that team's popularity draws more support.

But in an amateur sport high performance costs. In all its forms it costs money: the upkeep of such facilities and maintaining their standards, the cost of insurance and energy not to mention materials and specialised equipment, trained staff. All of that costs money. Building facilities that last and that provide high-quality facilities for athlete preparation is an expensive business.

There are other costs. High-performance facilities are also particularly specialised, catering for sportspeople who use and move through the facility in a particular way, something that requires imaginative design, integration, connectivity between different parts of the environment, consultation with the athletes, the input of the training staff. That adds up, but if corners are cut the result is empty rooms and dirty floors to go with the heating bills and maintenance costs.

To be fair to Tom Ryan, he took a balanced view of the phenomenon. He didn't agree that the centre of excellence is a proposition that is inherently over-ambitious for county boards, for instance.

'No, I don't think so. And you might level that charge more reasonably at other things that we traditionally have ploughed money into.

'First of all, I'm not mad about the term "centre of excellence" because there are connotations around that which I'm not fond of. One county recently designated theirs as a games development/centre of participation, and I thought that was great.

'What I'd like to see is a place which hosts something like what happened in Abbotstown recently, when I went out there for one of the football rules trial matches. You're sitting there with an interesting cross-section of people looking on at the matches and trying to learn a little bit, watching very high-profile players, some of the best in the country. And then over on the far pitch beyond that was a camogie game probably at under-twelve level, and I was thinking, "That's what it's supposed to be" – those girls are coming off their pitch the same time as Michael Murphy is walking off his pitch.'

Ryan acknowledged one of the main motivations for having a centre of excellence, a venue and facility that is not club-based:

'I think they have a huge value in practical terms because it's getting harder and harder to get places to play: the idea that they're located centrally and that it's somewhere that everybody converges upon, outside of the club, is very valuable and useful. The fact that there's no commercial aspect to those, it's not necessarily a bad thing.'

This led to an obvious question: should a county board be going millions of euros into the hole on such a facility, particularly when there might be an alternative?

'Then it gets interesting, because what is the county board there to do? Is it there to cultivate the next generation of players and to foster players of all ability and grades, and to promote a games programme that is going to run from the start to the end of the year and make sure that this playable facilities . . .

'Yes, it is something that they should do. And, like we know to our cost, you can't turn it into a commercial entity despite how you might try. On top of that you have to both pitch its use at a level that anyone can afford. Be careful that it's not the handy way out for those clubs that want to spare their own pitches!

'But we knew that getting into it; it doesn't have a commercial aspect to it, and for our part we can manage that. The point about the counties, you're wary that they are taking on a load that might well prove onerous, but to my mind, that's also what they're set up to do. The other stuff, the reason that a county should do the commercial stuff, is to give you a kind of free hand with the non-commercial, non-viable stuff – you're able to afford to do that.

'People might well express a bit of reservation about counties putting extra sponsors on their jersey sleeves, so now they've got three or four sponsors on the jerseys. And on the face of it, you'd be saying, "Yeah, is that really worth it? Is that a good thing? Are we going too far commercially?" And the fair and reasonable retort to that, I think, is that that's what allows us to do the other stuff that you're talking about – all the events and projects that are essential run on a loss.'

That's another angle on the GAA's property portfolio: that it's essentially unprofitable. The big house on Jones's Road is an outlier in that sense, with its concerts and conferencing business. As Ryan pointed out, the other stadiums aren't exactly overworked.

'Don't forget, you might level the same charge about profitability and centres of excellence at more traditional types of expenditure. There isn't a county ground in the country that makes a return, I'd say. Croke Park is probably the only one that really makes money, and that's based on exceptional circumstances too, for all sorts of reasons like concerts and the fact that it's in a city where there's a conference business.

'But Clones or Tuam or Nowlan Park or wherever, and these are all places where you are charging people an admission fee, it's still touch and go as regards whether they can operate as a reasonable surplus or even one that allows them to put aside funds for maintenance and for improvements when that time comes.

'And that is facing us as an organisation now. We're in a very fortunate position. We have significant assets and we have a significant presence around the country, but that brings with it a cost that is increasingly a challenge in terms of upkeep, and that's before you even think of the notion of having to replace these things or having to really future-proof them. There are two or three counties that don't have a county ground at all, and they face even more significant challenges of getting up and running with them.

'So I defend the idea of the centre of excellence or training centre. You go into them any day of the week, they're hopping with fifteen-year-olds and development squads and so on, they're hives of activity. I think they're great. But if you go into Tuam Stadium or another stadium on a Tuesday morning, not much is happening there.

'It's a valid question. Maybe we could level it up with other things.'

When it comes to the idea of a centre of excellence it's worth pointing out that partnerships are an obvious way to sidestep a massive capital project. Partnering up with a third- or second-level college in the county is a good way to offset costs if that option is available.

One size doesn't fit all, either. The centre of excellence for a county like Louth is going to be different to an equivalent facility in Cork, for instance. Declan McBennett says:

'The All-Ireland champions [Armagh] are building their new centre of excellence in Portadown, which is designed to be a model for football, hurling, camogie and ladies' football. If you look around the province Donegal already have theirs, Owenbeg is in Derry and Garvaghey in Tyrone. But Down don't have one, Armagh don't, Monaghan have one but to the best of my knowledge, Fermanagh don't have one. So even within the provinces, there are differentiations, just as within the counties there are massive differences. In Armagh Crossmaglen would have multiple pitches, Silverbridge multiple pitches, Dromintee multiple pitches. But you go to the north of the county and nobody has that level of facilities at play: they're dealing with different things. That feeds into where county teams train, where juvenile and minor teams train and lads have to get on a bus.

'My own son was playing for the Armagh minors and had to get on a bus at five o'clock to travel to training at the far end of the county and would get home at eleven o'clock at night – while trying to balance that with exams. Now that's what he wanted; he wanted to be a county minor. But where the facilities are is itself a challenge that's faced on an ongoing basis.'

When I mentioned the GAA's edifice complex being a potential landmine, McBennett picked up on the reference immediately.

'It's funny you use the word landmine there, because I think this is an historical, cultural, land-based issue that is in the Irish psyche: "We must have it and we must own it." I think if you go to Europe and you look at all the municipal facilities whereby you have multiple sports sharing the same facility, I think that's inevitable. I think it should happen, and I think it should have happened by now.

'The differentiation that I would make with regard to some of the centres of excellence is that that's the only way in rural counties that all Gaelic games – camogie, football, hurling and ladies' football – will be facilitated.

'I think the centre of excellence idea in terms of the four codes are brilliant. It doesn't include handball, obviously, but in terms of the four main codes it's brilliant, but it has to go both ways. I think from nine to five they should be used by the schools, and in the evening, the school funding should have the floodlights to allow the clubs to use the pitches, so that every-body is getting the maximum out of it. I was in Spain during the summer, in Alicante, and your basketball pitch and your hockey pitch is the same thing, which is also your soccer pitch. And everything is allocated. It's the one facility, the one funding allocation. It has to be done. I know Tom Ryan has suggested this in his last two reports, but everything is slower than it needs to be, and it needs to accelerate, and it needs to accelerate fast.'

As seen elsewhere in this book the municipal partnership model is one acknowledged across the GAA. The only question is how to organise the timetable, a question McBennett fielded like a man well used to scheduling a work roster.

'There's seven nights in the week, so Monday, Wednesday, Friday, Sunday, it belongs to X; Tuesday, Thursday, Saturday, it belongs to Y. It's the same as any fixture clashes that you see. There isn't a year that goes by that you're not writing about the LGFA and Camogie Association having teams going out to play on the same weekend or the same day.

'It requires sensible people with progressive brains to sit down at the same table and work it out and say, "Okay, we have this. How do we make the best use of it?" So the schools should be using the centre of excellence during the day for the school matches and training, while the clubs should be using the school pitches in the evening, when there's nobody at the school, and the cycle can work on that basis.

'Then the second part of that is what sport is being done, what part of the year is required for the seasons. Obviously we don't have the same climatic conditions as the Scandinavian countries, but you'll find in those that the municipal facilities that are used for soccer during the summer are used for ice hockey or other winter sports during the winter. So if they can figure it out, surely we have enough sensible people in Ireland who can sit down and figure it out.'

YOU WILL RESPECT MY (LOCAL) AUTHORITY – AND WORK TOGETHER

The relationship between the GAA and the government is a strange one. At times it breaks into open hostility. An issue like the GAAGO controversy is useful in that it points up an essential difference between the two but one that isn't always acknowledged. For all the communities it serves and its role in the country, the GAA is still focused on itself. This is a natural outlook and a logical one – it would be a strange organisation that didn't look out for its own good – but by virtue of being sectoral, the GAA's interests can cut across the government's from time to time. Sometimes the GAA can seem to cleave a little too closely to the old misquote of Charles Wilson, once boss of General Motors: 'What's good for General Motors is good for America,' but substituting 'GAA' and 'Ireland' in the obvious places.

What might be more interesting to look at is the GAA's relationship with local and municipal authorities. These are the bodies its constituent elements are likely to interact with more regularly, though when I started this book I thought the municipal partnership model was a fairly radical move for the GAA.

To go into partnership with local authorities would have implications in terms of ceding control and autonomy, something no organisation in Ireland has ever accepted without gritting its teeth. Hence the strangeness of the prospect of the GAA actually agreeing to, for example, the announcement in

November 2024 by Brendan Smith, TD for Cavan-Monaghan, of the new €19 million Cavan Regional Sports Hub, which was to receive funding under the government's LSSIF:

> This complex will provide a covered sports arena with playing pitch, spectator seating, and other ancillary accommodation. The Sports Centre Building will have changing facilities, multi-purpose rooms, reception and ancillary accommodation. There will be four GAA fields, synthetic hockey/multi-sport pitch, cricket practice area/catch nets and all facilities with lighting.
>
> This project is being provided by Cavan County Council, Cavan GAA and the Royal School and I strongly commend their work and commitment to this fabulous project which will be of huge significance to our region.

At around the same time Cuala GAA club issued the following statement:

> Cuala GAA is delighted to have been informed that the Hyde Park Community Sports Centre Project has been granted €4.6m towards the construction cost through the Government's Large Scale Sports Infrastructure Fund (LSSIF) . . . Completion of this project will help to address the sports infrastructure deficit in the area and provide enhanced indoor sports and social facilities for Cuala members and project partners Dalkey United and St John of God's Adult Services.

Not all the GAA applications were successful. Tipperary GAA made an application for funding under the LSSIF to go towards redeveloping the stadium's Kinane Stand but had also come together with Tennis Ireland seeking financial assistance for the multi-sport complex at Technological University of the Shannon Thurles. Significantly enough, the latter project was approved by Tipperary County Council but both failed to get LSSIF funding.

Despite the disappointment in Knocknagow, the municipal partnership model is less a radical suggestion than an integral part of the GAA's plans moving forward, it seems. Ger Ryan of the Munster Council certainly thought so:

'It must be on the table in terms of the future . . . the GAA community is wonderful to build and raise funds to build. But raising funds to maintain a place – it's a different proposition; there isn't the same energy around that, there isn't the same commitment. I always give the example of your own house. If you build your house you spend a few bob every year to maintain it, obviously. A stadium is a hundred houses. You have to do the same thing, but people forget about that. They say it's there and you actually don't have to do anything with it, but whether it's used or unused, it has to be maintained.

'And we have to understand what we are investing in. Does it make sense and is it the best use of money for us?

'Sometimes facilities are available through the education sector, and that's another important partner, potentially. Recently we had a case of a county trying to build facilities when they could rent the same facilities from a college, with sufficient access for their needs for forty years – for the same money. Why would you try to raise that money up front?

'It's time to change that mindset, that it has to be ours, we must own it and we must be almost competing to the exclusion of other sports. I don't see sharing facilities as an issue because our product and how we look after people and how we're community based and if we can maintain the volunteers, to me, they're all strong enough to be able to maintain the core of the GAA. Where's the GAA in five, ten years' time? It still has to be built on a model of voluntarism and be community based – but there are different communities.'

Ryan warmed to his theme:

'Communities are different. Thirty years ago, we probably knew everybody in our community, urban or rural, but that's not the case with either urban or rural settings now, and here's just a whole different self-sufficiency in terms of how you operate. There isn't that same interdependence. We have to build a different community model, which has been done very successfully in the big urban clubs, we have a great model of that.

'The next challenge is integration, not just integration between the three associations, but also integration of the new communities we have in Ireland, the new people who don't have historical connections in Ireland. It's great to see those communities represented on teams now, and that's also important.'

Ryan's remarks on municipal partnerships were echoed wholeheartedly by Croke Park's Peter McKenna.

'I think it's inevitable. As an organisation we have invested heavily in facilities in a way some other organisations have not. Others have invested in players and other activities, which makes the bleating a bit hollow when that starts.

'I think it's inevitable that the government will look at funding municipal venues around the country. The Bekan Dome was a good example, something with utility regardless of the weather and applicable to all sports. Perhaps the government should look at putting twelve, sixteen, twenty of those in strategic locations all over Ireland for various sports, with the facilities being shared.

'On a side issue, I think government funding allocations for sport should sometimes be done on a more strategic basis, bringing sports together to ask, "What makes sense for all sports here? It's taxpayer money, so how can we get the best return on it?"'

Dublin is a good test case, as it happens. McKenna points to a couple of municipal ventures in the capital that didn't work out for the GAA.

'I look up the road from the office and the new Phibsborough stadium project is a great idea but it's too small for Gaelic games. The same with the Tallaght stadium, too small for Gaelic games. Those were funded by Dublin City Council but they exclude Gaelic games. I don't think that's a deliberate thing, I think there were considerations around the size of the site that had an effect, but there does need to be a long-term plan for sport on the island of Ireland, a fifty-year plan, maybe?'

At a more immediate level there's the relationship with the local authority. In some counties it's good, in some it's non-existent. And in some there can be a lingering sense of unfairness. When the Aviva Stadium hosted the Georgia Tech–Florida State college football game in 2024 a couple of observers pointed to the extent of the authorities' welcome for the supporters, down to a fan zone in Temple Bar, comparing it to the low-key accommodation of the All-Ireland finals and semi-finals every summer. Could more be done to create a carnival atmosphere on those weekends by the local authorities in Dublin? Peter McKenna agreed, though 'in a slightly qualified way'.

'Our games have a rhythm and American football is very different. People come early to the games, they'll tailgate outside, the game itself is very long; all in all it can be an eight-hour experience. With us, people travel up to the game, have a bite to eat in the stadium, see the game and then head home. It's a very different rhythm. So we don't have that same sense of gathering en masse that you'd have at American football, though there are some pretty obvious exceptions.

'Thurles is the obvious example, where the Square hosts everyone before they all decant to the stadium. And we saw a bit of that with the All-Ireland club finals recently, where Cuala and Na Fianna both marched up to the stadium almost like a band of warriors, which was great.

'To be fair, I wouldn't knock the city on the welcome for American football. What I would say is the tour buses in the city don't come to Croke Park, perhaps because it's seen as slightly inconvenient, though the stadium is a huge attraction. To me Croke Park feeds into the narrative that coming to Ireland isn't just about Guinness – much as we like it – that there's a different offering available here.'

On a more routine level McKenna points to certain other issues that Croke Park raises from time to time and some that might be common to other large GAA venues around the country. It isn't being hyper-sensitive to ask, for instance, if those venues are taken for granted in those areas.

'Where this all becomes an issue is that it costs us a fortune to open the gates of the stadium. We pay €1.2 million in rates, probably another seven hundred thousand in Garda costs, another seven hundred thousand in street cleaning and washing and so forth. Add all of that up, and it means that before we get one person through the gates of the stadium we have approximately three million in outgoings that need to be made back.

'I think there's a more creative way of looking at that. For instance, do we really need to be responsible for paying rates at that level, given we're bringing people into the city?'

There are ready-made comparisons.

'The golf in Portmarnock is going to get, I think, a forty million push to make it happen. I don't doubt the Ryder Cup will be supported to make it happen. The Europa Cup game here [German side Bayer Leverkusen and Italy's Atalanta played in that competition's final at the Aviva in May 2024] was almost eight million in Garda costs. For one game.

'The point I'm making is that sometimes something becomes wallpaper or so obvious it's not noticed any more. Our activities in Croke Park, and in Cork, in Thurles, Clones, Galway, every-where, can be forgotten in terms of what it means to those towns and cites, in terms of the people being pulled into those places to enjoy themselves and to spend money in those places.

'The Ryder Cup isn't paying rates. American football isn't paying rates. I'm in favour of those coming to Ireland for all sorts of reasons, but I'd also be in favour of us getting a break on the centralised charges being laid upon us. And I'd include the Aviva and the 3 Arena and all of those in that as well, abso-lutely, not just us.'

It should be pointed out, in addition, that Croke Park and other GAA stadiums are offering another service which is often overlooked. At a time when urban dereliction, traffic and trans-port issues, and antisocial behaviour are being blamed for people withdrawing from town and city centres, those venues pull thousands of people into those same urban centres.

On the face of it that looks like a powerful argument for some flexibility with rates, given the spending generated by those match attendees. In an ideal world the revenue generated in that way would even stay within the local authority's pockets, but that's a whole other complication.

PART 6
FUTURE

THE GAELIC PART OF THE GAA

The Athletic element of the name explains itself pretty quickly. The Association part the same. What about the Gaelic part? The GAA came about in the very age of the Celtic Twilight, when matters of Irish culture and identity came to the fore. Sometimes it can appear that the Gaelic element of the GAA is confined to a few rote phrases delivered at trophy presentations. Sometimes it can be a lot more.

'Ours is the only Gaeltacht in the country where the daily number of Irish speakers has increased over two consecutive censuses, and the most important organisation, I believe, in this area, is the GAA club.'

That was Irial Mac Murchú, talking about the GAA and the Gaeltacht in west Waterford centred on An Rinn. The club he mentioned is Rinn Ó gCuanach.

'It's the biggest and most deeply rooted and one that has tentacles in almost every house in the area, and it's run entirely in Irish. So whether you have your first taste of the club at Cúl Camp time in the summer, when you're a small child, and try and rise up to intermediate hurling and senior football, it is a huge hold for the language, and if that were to be taken away from us, or in any way impacted, that would be a huge blow to the language here.

'And that is one of the reasons why it would be a desperate measure if we came to the conclusion that there needs to be an amalgamation. It is pivotal, and it's really, really important.

That's not to say we don't have trainers in from time to time who don't speak Irish, and then the dressing room language changes temporarily to English and all of that. But the soul of the club is *as Gaeilge*.'

Wearing his hat as CEO of Nemeton, of course, Irish is the medium through which Mac Murchú's company works, delivering coverage of Gaelic games and more. Could the GAA be more proactive, do more for Irish?

'I don't think the GAA gets enough credit for what it does for Irish. You have had successive presidents – Pat Fanning from Waterford, Peter Quinn, Nickey Brennan, Liam O'Neill, Aogán Ó Fearghail, Joe McDonagh, Jarlath Burns – God knows who I've left out – each and every one of them has been a fluent Irish speaker. There has always been an approach in the marketing department towards doing things bilingually and always looking for clever devices not to lessen the impact of an advert that way.

'Jamie Ó Tuama is a very good Irish language officer in Croke Park. Alan Milton, the head of communications there, is very good; I don't know if Tom Ryan is a gaeilgeoir, but he's certainly supportive. They might get a bad rap at times but I don't know if it's deserved.

'The announcements in Croke Park are bilingual. The big screen material (which we produce) is bilingual. Most scoreboards and games right throughout the country are in Irish, though I see a drift towards English. People don't seem to be aware of the by-law that says that teams have to be named in Irish. The onus on the GAA, once upon a time, in terms of television matches, was that the minor would be in Irish and the senior would be in English.

'I think the GAA have been very loyal to TG4 over the years, and I think that they have stuck with TG4, and I think it's been mutually beneficial for the GAA, for TG4 and for the language. Looking back, the GAA did not need to be as loyal to TG4 as it has been, even though it was mutually beneficial. And the benefit of that, the manifestation of that, is in the fact that anyone who is now touching forty has never known anything except the games being in Irish on television.

'So this thing that we had in the early days – "Why isn't the commentary in English?" – doesn't even arise. People just by osmosis soak in the language every Sunday listening to our commentators. I think that has had a huge impact, and you have to give some of the credit of that to the GAA as well as TG4.'

Further west, Dara Ó Cinnéide of Raidió na Gaeltachta and An Ghaeltacht club in west Kerry has another perspective on the language.

'As an organisation we're too big to be as clearly defined as we were, say, in 1884. To me the Gaelic part of the Gaelic Athletic Association has been long forgotten – that's a cultural thing. As players it's a debate we would have had back in our twenties, when myself and the Ó Sés would have been travelling in the car to matches. In our club it's "*spioraid, croí, caid agus teanga*" – the language is very important. But I remember having chats with Darragh (Ó Sé) and he'd be asking, 'What are we really?' Those chats would be in English, by the way, though I'd have always chatted to his brother Fergal in Irish, but Darragh would ask, 'Does it really matter what language we talk in the dressing room, should we not be all about developing players?'

'Now, twenty years or more after those conversations, I think we're all coming to certain conclusions. The Gaelic element of the GAA is going to be in trouble anyway, so really what we're about is being a community organisation which is trying to get as many players as possible, boys and girls, playing – and by playing I mean the one sport we play, Gaelic football. And not being focused on the level of your ability at that game so much as developing players and giving them an outlet.

'The language and the cultural element is not as strong as it was twenty-five, thirty, forty years ago: we wouldn't be good on Scór, for instance, we're a Gaelic football club.'

It was interesting to note, of course, that Ó Cinnéide himself gave one of the greatest victory speeches in Irish when he collected Sam Maguire for Kerry: his bona fides when it comes to the language are beyond question. His focus on what his club offers centres not on the possibility that people might find the language a barrier but on the possibilities open even to the casual visitor.

'Our area is vast but not densely populated, and the club is a place for you. We don't have a clubhouse, but you can visit and have a cup of tea; if you want to walk around the grounds we'll put on the lights for you. If you're down around the area on your summer holidays and you or the kids want to come in to the field and kick around, or puck around, that's not a problem.'

Is it preferable to stress the Association part of the GAA rather than the Gaelic element? Having the gates open if a couple of kids want to come in and billow the nets is a potent declaration, one visible to all. Maybe the Irish part can come later, once you have them on the grounds.

The significance of the Gaelic part of the GAA shouldn't be understated, however. The organisation was founded on certain core principles, and rule 4 of its official guide is pretty clear: 'The Association shall actively support the Irish language, traditional Irish dancing, music, song, and other aspects of Irish culture. It shall foster an awareness and love of the national ideals in the people of Ireland, and assist in promoting a community spirit through its clubs.'

Granted, that's easier said than defined. What Irish culture may mean to one member of a GAA club may be unrecognisable as culture in a club two miles up the road, never mind in another province.

But it would be dangerous to leave the Gaelic part up on the top shelf. All things considered, Irial Mac Murchú's view seems to be on the right track: the GAA's support for Irish in the last thirty years, roughly since TG4 was created, which is no coincidence, has been more than lip service, certainly. That augurs well.

AN END TO REFERENCES

The GAA's involvement with local issues isn't always positive.

In 2021 a man convicted of raping a woman while she slept in her own bed had several character references provided for him. Conor Quaid was convicted at the Central Criminal Court and sentenced to eight years, with 18 months suspended. In one of those character references, John Diony O'Connor spoke highly of Quaid's good character and his commitment to Dingle GAA. O'Connor said later he had offered the testimonial in a personal capacity. He was not an officer of Dingle GAA club when he wrote the reference, though he became vice-chairman of the club afterwards. He wasn't the only one to provide a character reference either – a publican and a retired Garda sergeant did the same – but O'Connor's comments were specifically focused on Quaid's Gaelic games pedigree, referring to his commitment to the Dingle GAA and stating that he had always played as a team player since underage.

The victim's family complained to Kerry GAA and its response was that O'Connor's reference was given in a personal capacity. Mr O'Connor's testimonial did not suggest it reflected the views of the Dingle club, county secretary Peter Twiss responded to the family of the victim, and he offered his heartfelt thoughts to the family and the victim.

Vera O'Leary, director of the Kerry Rape and Sexual Abuse Centre, disagreed with the GAA's assertion that the reference was made in a personal capacity, telling the *Examiner* at the time:

Diony O'Connor is very influential in the GAA. There is a lack of understanding. This case was strongly contested. He has never shown remorse for his crime.

Victim impact statements have to be approved by the court and accepted by all sides before they are allowed to be delivered; the same standards should be applied in the criminal justice system to character references. A victim impact statement has clear guidelines – glowing character references should also. We would be willing to do training with the GAA on victim consciousness, sensitivity and awareness around the issue of sexual violence.

O'Leary was absolutely correct, and the force of her argument is supported by the GAA's own guidelines.

The GAA's Code of Conduct (clause 4.3.4.3) says that GAA members must not:

provide any form of character reference for an individual as part of legal or Court Proceedings, in his or her capacity as an Officer of the GAA (if applicable). For the avoidance of doubt, GAA Participants may not use GAA-related letterhead nor sign any such character reference in their capacity as an Officer of the GAA. Furthermore, any character reference, whether provided by an Officer or a Member should specify that it is being provided in a personal capacity and not in anyway on behalf of or as an Officer or a Member of the GAA.

That seems reasonably clear when it comes to character references that are part of the sentencing process in criminal law. Once the defendant has been found or pleaded guilty, character references are supplied by those who know the defendant, effectively to plead in mitigation of sentence. In giving a character reference, a person is not condoning the criminal behaviour of the person but speaking about their character as that person knows them. Legal experts often say that character references are just one small part of what the judge must take into account and the weight that a judge gives them varies. The victim will also give a victim impact statement and juxtaposing this statement (and the trauma and experiences of the victim) against what the defendant's supporters say is so 'out of character' for the defendant it is sometimes jarring, especially in sexual offences cases.

When Mickey Harte was appointed Derry senior football manager in 2023 the advocacy group Alliance for Choice Derry issued a hard-hitting statement on his selection. The group cited a 2010 sexual assault on a woman in Derry by a Tyrone man, Ronan McCusker:

> This woman was found unconscious in a laneway some hours later by two men on their way to work. At first, the men thought they had discovered a dead body due to her condition. At Derry Crown Court, Judge Piers Grant described McCusker's offending behaviour as, 'extremely wicked', and added that he had 'taken advantage of a vulnerable woman'.
>
> Having survived this attack, this woman subsequently endured weaponised misogyny aimed at her by Mickey Harte, who provided a character reference for McCusker during his trial. Harte stated that McCusker came from a 'good GAA family' and pleaded for leniency in his sentencing . . . These actions directly led to McCusker being sentenced for a mere 30 months (15 months suspended).

Alliance for Choice quoted a Rape Crisis Centre statement from March 2013, which condemned:

> the appalling decision of Mickey Harte to provide a character reference for the dangerous sex attacker who has shown not one iota of remorse for his disgusting crime. Sadly, we cannot ignore the distinct possibility that the astounding decision of Mr Harte's to provide a character reference had a direct, material effect on the judge's disgracefully lenient sentence which was handed out to the offender.
>
> Mickey Harte's unapologetic and continued support of a convicted sex offender means he should not be given the honour of representing the Oak Leaf county as a Manager.

Eamonn McCann of *Hot Press* found the woman who was assaulted and interviewed her for that magazine. He found that she, too, was from a 'GAA family' and she told McCann:

> Mickey Harte is a man so many of us looked up to, as an ambassador and an inspiration for young players. But he spoke up for the person who attacked me even after he pleaded guilty. What was he thinking? Maybe he was misinformed.
>
> But he had a chance to withdraw and say sorry, say he didn't realise the extent of what I had been put through. But he didn't do that . . . I don't think his reference for this man reflected well on the GAA . . . At first, I wouldn't go down to the GAA club, but I go down now. I did think that people were looking at me, judging me, and I didn't know how to handle it.

Clearly problems arise when people give character references and claim to be doing so in a personal capacity. It's surprising that m'learned friends have not focused their minds more closely on teasing out the difference between personal and semi-official capacities, but that kind of analysis shouldn't be necessary. As noted, the GAA's guidelines on the subject are so unambiguous it's difficult to see how prominent members of the Association still issue such character references.

To be fair, the GAA has also worked actively in this space. Game Changer, a partnership between the GAA, Ruhama and White Ribbon Ireland supported by the LGFA and Camogie Associations, seeks to raise awareness and action through sport to tackle domestic, sexual and gender-based violence.

The three-year project is supported by governmental funding through Cuan and is designed to deliver on the objectives of the government's Third National Strategy on Domestic, Sexual, and Gender-Based Violence.

The 'awareness' mentioned above is a key term. If it's fair to say that it's been lacking in some of the cases where character references have been given, it's visible in other contexts. For instance, when Dublin's great midfielder Michael Darragh McAuley spoke to *Off the Ball* on Newstalk about the grotesque misogynist Andrew Tate, his dismissal of Tate was leavened with advice on how to broach the subject.

> It's missed my generation a bit. Lads in their thirties are more at home with themselves and probably found whatever their version of masculinity is, and Andrew Tate hasn't been a big factor in our lives. It's only recently that we started talking about him. And it is worrying when you start talking to the younger people and start talking to people in their teens and Andrew Tate is big noise. People are believing what he's saying. Anyone who is spouting views like that it has to be clocked and watched.

You have to be very careful how you speak about it because at that age, if you tell me not to listen to someone, I'm going to listen to them even more and I'd buy their T-shirt too, I would have been that kid. So it needs to be explained and talked through why people are listening to this dude so people have an understanding where these views are coming from and what nonsense it is.

That's the example the GAA should be giving. Not offering character references for rapists.

SPEED BUMPS AHEAD. OR SERIOUS OBSTACLES?

When I ask Anthony O'Connor about changes in the culture, he nudges the conversation towards challenges involving substance abuse.

'A potential issue for us, in a roundabout way, is performance-enhancing drugs [PEDs]. There were articles in the recent past about PEDs and doping in schools rugby, and, particularly in our part of the world, our boys and girls go to rugby-playing schools in the area. So because of our geography, where we're located, we'd be very naive to think that that culture stops at the door of the GAA club and doesn't bleed into the football and hurling dressing room.

'Last year I organised a talk on drugs and sport here in our clubhouse, with great speakers, but there was no real uptake. I think it's important that we need to be getting front and centre in that space with young people to help them understand the dangers of this.'

GAA players aren't turning up too many positive tests for PEDs. Is that grounds for optimism? Some past Olympic Games, which looked clean on the surface because of the lack of positive tests, are now regarded, in retrospect, as utterly compromised because of subsequent revelations.

'Look at the physique of players now, their athleticism. I'd often look at pictures from the early 2000s and late nineties, and they'd all have the baggy jerseys on them. Haunches, the odd paunch. Now they're absolutely chiselled. I think sometimes we maybe overplay the virtue of ourselves. It's not as though we're immune to all these things that come with gym culture, for one thing, and the pressure now, at a young age, to get onto the county development squads, that treadmill – I think we'd be very naive to feel that our young people aren't tempted like that.

'As for PEDs, what does the testing look like? First, I can understand the opinion that a testing regime like this for amateur players is overkill. I can definitely empathise with that. But the rules for PEDs are there first and foremost to protect players. Obviously the integrity of a sport is important, but protecting the player, the fair player, is paramount to me. I think there should be some sort of compromise. I don't know how likely it is that a player will go through his or her career at inter-county level without being tested. Testing is imperfect but it's the best tool or weapon we have.'

Until an amateur gets caught up in the maelstrom? O'Connor offers a good example:

'The other side of that testing regime is you have a situation like Aidan O'Mahony's, when his case came up. He was cleared but he got dragged through that situation, which must have been incredibly stressful and harsh, particularly for a man in the position of a garda. That was very tough.'

Not all substances are performance-enhancing, of course. There is a great urban legend of an inter-county team retiring to their dressing room after an intense championship game some years ago when a knock came on the door: please produce players X and Y for mandatory Irish Sports Council drugs tests. Mr X volunteered without a fuss but Mr Y refused point blank, and after some delicate negotiations he murmured that he had some material in his system which was . . . ah . . . recreational in nature. At this point the legend usually dissolves into unverifiable conjecture.

Marina Hyde and Richard Osman might sound like odd bedfellows for a book about the future of Gaelic games, but one exchange in an episode of their *The Rest is Entertainment* podcasts struck a chord. They were discussing heckling at comedy gigs and wondered if there were particular reasons why audiences were so unruly. Did the audience have unrealistic expectations of the gig? Was it a hangover from the pandemic in that attendees simply didn't understand general gig etiquette? Was it because of the growth of parasocial relationships everywhere? Or was there something else entirely, something a little more sinister?

'A couple of comics said, interestingly, that cocaine has become a big thing in comedy audiences,' said Osman. 'Like in football crowds, it's huge,' said Hyde, and Osman agreed: 'Like in football crowds. And it becomes a big issue because there is no speaking to that person. That person does not know they're in a dialogue.'

The travails of a comedian trying to reason with a coke-addled audience member can only be guessed at, but Osman and Hyde raised an interesting point about crowd behaviour and drug use.

We're regularly told that cocaine is everywhere in Ireland, with its influence supposedly discernible everywhere, from wedding celebrations where the guests troop to the toilets for regular refreshment to the anecdotal rise in dangerous and selfish driving on our roads. Surely sport isn't exempt from that? The available evidence certainly supports that assumption.

In March 2024 the Dublin District Court heard the case of a Gaelic football fan caught with a bag of suspected cocaine at an All-Ireland semi-final at Croke Park. The man 'panicked' and swallowed it when gardaí approached. The court was told that a garda approached the man concerned and told him he would be searched, whereupon the man placed the bag into his mouth and swallowed it. He was arrested and duly faced the music in court.

High-profile players have also acknowledged cocaine use. Westmeath footballer Luke Loughlin outlined his addiction issues, which included cocaine, on RTÉ:

It progressed over time. It started off with alcohol, I obviously had mental health problems that I was never able to address. It progressed over time and I needed something stronger. Why I was doing it was because I probably wasn't able to deal with what was going on in my life and I needed to get high or drunk to face the problems that I had.

Eventually a video circulated of Loughlin asleep next to a train track:

I was obviously asleep, but God knows what was going through my head. I was after being on a coke binge for like two months, but this had been four days without sleep. God knows what was going on. People were obviously looking for me. That was where I had got to. That was my norm.

On the same programme Loughlin's mother Oonagh said:

You can go to any pub now and get it so easy. It's literally like getting a bag of sweets, it's crazy, to be honest . . . Literally every second person's cousin is a drug dealer now or has contacts to a coke dealer or something. It is very easy got.

The intersection of alcohol and cocaine use is significant. Clare referee Pat Byrne-O'Connell told *Newstalk* in February

2024 that he could see the growth in cocaine use from his vantage point in the pub industry, saying cocaine was 'out of control' in Ireland.

It's in every club in every county in every corner of Ireland. Anyone that thinks it's not is totally lost and blind. It's out of control and it's the GAA's own fault; they've created this monster by introducing what's called the alcohol ban.

All these coaches coming in, who know little or nothing about the social life of young people, banning alcohol. So the lads are coming to the pub, sitting at the bar counter with their 0.0 alcohol bottle perched in front of them, off their face on cocaine. That's what they're doing because you can't be seen to be drinking in the GAA any more. They're young fellas, they're social fellas, they're out with their friends at the weekends and that's what they're doing.

Anyone that says it's not happening is either blind or stupid, and I don't think there's many stupid people involved in the GAA. They've turned their back on it because it's the easy way out.

O'Byrne-O'Connell spelt out the procedure:

I have lads coming in from training and coming in from matches [saying], 'Pat, give me €100 cashback.' They go down straight to their 'friend', get their €100, hand it over, into the toilet and come up to the bar counter [for] a 0.0.

That's what they're doing in every club in the county, and not one club can say that it's not happening because it is. I would say one in two players in every club is taking cocaine on a weekly basis. It's every pub, it's every house party, it's everywhere. If you went down and did a drug test at a GAA match every weekend, you would capture at least one fella with cocaine in his system. It's easier to get drugs than drink.

Players using a pub to get an illegal drug while consuming a non-alcoholic beer must be one of the most on-the-nose ironies imaginable. Byrne-O'Connell's point about an alcohol ban being imposed by coaches – which is purely for the optics – while players are doing more damage to their bodies with cocaine is another contradiction in terms, one which is compounded when that alcohol ban is lifted.

Luke Loughlin also made this point in his contribution to RTÉ. 'When you maybe win or lose something, it could be a few months since you had a drink, and it's a blow up, you party as hard as you can.' And the drinking binge after a game – the famous 'Monday club' – can obviously include drugs.

Anthony O'Connor, wearing his GAA officer's and doctor's hats says:

'It's a problem that comes into the club from the outside, I guess, and I suppose what goes on in the clubs is reflective of that. For me, it's not just young people, it's more about fellas in their forties coming out of bathrooms and I'm thinking, "Christ, if you need that . . ."

'I think the way people socialise has changed anyway; the nightlife in the city or whatever has changed. And that shows in different ways. I would say what we're taking in in our clubhouse bar now is about half of what we took in ten years ago. Young people just don't drink any more in general, but they certainly seem to be doing an awful lot of cocaine. And [it's] not just the young people that are doing it, of course.

'It's a big problem in terms of preparation for games and so on, that obviously is bad news, but a young athlete might feel that if they're going to indulge in some substance on a rare night out, that in terms of their physical prowess perhaps taking cocaine might be a better option for them in some ways – "There's no calories in cocaine," that kind of thinking. I've never used cocaine myself, but I'm told that people believe they don't get the hangover as much as you would from a lot of drink. I think that's another big part of it. Young people are conscious of their calories, for one thing, and also – and people don't think of it this way – it's probably cheaper to get cocaine than drink to send your nervous system to the places you might want it to go.'

Mind you, drink still has its position in GAA celebrations. Many readers will be familiar, for instance, with the 'Monday Club' phenomenon, even if they themselves are not part of any such gathering. For the uninitiated, when a hurling or football team wins a championship, the players often take a couple of days off to celebrate, meeting up on the Monday in a neighbourhood bar. What's interesting, as O'Connor pointed out, is that social media can now bring some of those Monday celebrations right to your phone.

'I feel a little sorry for our athletes in many ways that the drinking can be very much glorified in other sports sometimes, and our athletes are supposed to behave like monks. I think a lot of it has to do with how media is consumed as well. You see players from whatever club, they had a big win, and here's the Monday Club, it's being celebrated. In fairness, lads are entitled to celebrate and to enjoy themselves, but there are teams who've gotten themselves into trouble along the way, such as the team in Kilkenny [St Patrick's (Ballyragget)] that got a few ladies in to help celebrate a win couple of years ago.

'A lot of the time everybody has a laugh and they move on, but lives are troubled by this stuff, too. If you look at a video of thirty or forty lads drinking on a Monday morning after winning a trophy, some of those lads are going to be problem drinkers. Those are the stats. And yes, it's not just GAA, or even just sport, you'll have those kinds of percentages in any group of drinkers, but glorifying it . . . it's very difficult to find a balance. I've had some great nights myself with teams.

'On the whole, sport is one of the best protectors in keeping people away from dangerous substances. And I think, in fairness, the GAA has shown a lot of leadership in this. In my opinion it has probably done more than a lot of the other big bodies have in this regard, and one area in which they've shown huge leadership is in gambling. That's a massive problem and I think they can be proud of a lot of what they've done in that space.

'Is there more that could be done? I'm not really sure there is, because as long as matches have been won teams and players will celebrate that. But I'm not that comfortable with the Monday Club thing being put out as content, if you like.'

The 'Is team drinking bonding or blackguarding?' debate seems to be simmering since the Middle Ages across almost every team sport, and there's no need to rehash the bullet points in this wearyingly familiar discussion. It's worth acknowledging, however, that a hurling or football team hitting the pub on a Monday and broadcasting its high jinks to all and sundry presents a couple of challenging questions.

For instance, the sight may be discomfiting for some, but it's also fair to say these are young men enjoying themselves in an entirely legal, open manner in their free time. They don't have employment contracts with morality clauses; there's no question of financial penalties for bringing their club into disrepute. They're celebrating a pastime, not a profession. All of which leads back to a question raised earlier. When do GAA players become role models? Or are they role models to begin with?

FIXTURES DON'T OCCUR IN A VACUUM

Nothing kills a GAA chat like fixture scheduling. In *GAAconomics* I described it as a conversation killer, and the judgement stands. As a topic it has extraordinary entertainment-retardant qualities. Which is a pity in one way, because arranging fixtures can sometimes resemble four-dimensional chess. There are so many factors to be considered, from the religious calendar to traditional employment patterns, that it can be extraordinarily difficult to schedule even one inter-county game to maximise its attraction and accessibility.

Take this test case. Kerry played Monaghan in the All-Ireland qualifiers on 18 May 2024 at Fitzgerald Stadium, with throw-in fixed for 3 p.m. Don't worry if you're struggling to recall the precise details of the encounter. It was no classic. Kerry won 0–24 to 1–11. They led by 13 points at the break, when Monaghan had managed just the two points in an entire half of football. The visitors' late goal only slapped some respectability on the final result, and at the final whistle all involved quickly packed their bags for the next stop on the championship merry-go-round.

If the quality on show between the white lines hasn't burnt itself in the memory, why focus on this game? It stands as a test case of the challenges of fixture scheduling, a perfect example of how planning match dates and throw-in times intersects with real life and how that in turn impacts on attendances.

The radio commentators for the game passed comment, for instance, on the low attendance, which was officially recorded at 8,092. It seems at first glance quite low, even in comparison with that year's Munster final a couple of weeks previously; there was plenty of room in Cusack Park in Ennis for that one – it drew just 12,000 paying spectators through the turnstiles. The commentators also referred to the Kerry County Board's decision to fix a round of senior football league games for that evening as militating against a large home attendance.

This was a fair point. Kerry is a very large county, and it would be perfectly understandable if supporters from the western end of the Dingle peninsula, for instance, opted to see An Ghaeltacht, their local club, in a league game at the home pitch in Gallarus that evening rather than driving over an hour to Killarney for the county game and then back again.

Consider that experience duly replicated in other remote parts of the county, south and north. Add in the durable perception that Kerry people reserve the right to travel to support their county until the knock-out stages of the All-Ireland series, a perception buttressed by decades of hard evidence. But don't forget either about the eight-hour round trip facing any Monaghan person who was looking to take in the game. No matter how passionate you are about your team, that kind of journey makes you swallow hard.

Best not to get into the championship structure which meant that a home win more or less guaranteed Kerry's progress to the next stage, which rather undercut any sense of cut-throat competition and which obliterated any sense of followers feeling it was absolutely necessary to be there in case it was the last game their county played in that year's championship. If we focus on that we'll get seriously sidetracked, so let's look instead at the fact that there are some wider issues at play with a 3 p.m. throw-in. On a Saturday. In May. In Kerry.

Kerry isn't the only county in Ireland that relies heavily on tourism, but to go by the Kerry County Council website it's hard to think of another county quite as focused on looking after its visitors:

> Kerry currently attracts 13% of all overseas visitors to Ireland and one in three American visitors includes Kerry on their itineraries. It has the greatest concentration of tourist accommodation outside of Dublin – up to 50,000 beds in the approved and unapproved sectors.
>
> Kerry is also more dependent on tourism than any other county with over 20% of its workforce employed in tourism-related enterprises and has over 9,000 people directly employed in the accommodation and hospitality sectors.

The bland statement about accommodation and hospitality can be read another way: weekend work is a huge part of life in Kerry. The tourism industry is centred on catering to people who are enjoying their free time, and for many people, of course, time is never freer than it is at the weekend. As a consequence, it's fair to conclude that a sizeable proportion of the 20 per cent of the workforce mentioned by Kerry County Council simply couldn't make that game against Monaghan even if they wanted to. They were working in the middle of the afternoon when it was played.

Tourism facilities in the Kingdom were probably in higher demand that weekend than they had been in several months. Readers with good memories may recall that that was the first real splash of sunshine in the summer, with temperatures crawling into the low twenties for the first time in 2024: more demands on the tourism industry, from hospitality to accommodation to less prominent aspects of the sector.

Another complication arose that had nothing to do with the quality of the game or ticket prices. May is Holy Communion month all over Ireland, and schools from Kilgarvan to Blennerville had classes trooping down to their parish churches that Saturday and singing 'Queen of the May' as they went. That took other potential spectators out of the running to attend the Monaghan game; for all the decline in church attendance, a First Communion is still an event of significance for many families. Enough significance to reduce the importance of a football match, certainly.

As for the array of club games and their impact on attendances, it's worth pointing out one more salient fixture. The All-Ireland under-twenty football final was played in Portlaoise the following day, with Kerry taking on Tyrone. Obviously those scheduling the Sam Maguire fixtures months beforehand can't tell the future, but it presented something of a dilemma to the Kerry football fan, one complicated by basic economics. In the current climate – any climate, really – travelling to two inter-county games in one weekend is a major financial commitment. Given the choice between a relatively mundane senior fixture and an All-Ireland final a couple of hours' drive up the motorway, how many picked the latter? How many *could* pick the latter given their work commitments? How many shrugged their shoulders and decided to nip to the local field for a senior league game, maybe after a day in church for a Holy Communion?

Readers will immediately spot the most significant factors here. There was a time, a very recent era, when May was a time of provincial championship clashes, not All-Ireland series games, but that was before the introduction of the famous split season, which compressed the playing calendar to facilitate club and county players alike. That has led in turn to a good deal of discussion of the impact of the split season on broadcasting, match attendances, training loads – take your pick.

But is there a more important takeaway here? About dwindling attraction?

* * *

When does the alarm bell sound? We've seen in this book the value of the long view, and often those in power within the GAA can apply some perspective and damp down any sudden blaze of overreaction. But some concerns are harder to bat away. Irial Mac Murchú identified 'a few of them off the top of my head', pointing to rising costs as an obvious opener.

'The general expense required, not just to run the GAA as an organisation but each county. Nobody bats an eyelid any more when they hear that a county senior hurling or football team ran into seven figures. There was shock horror twenty years ago when people moved to seven figures.

'What is going to keep funding that? The sponsorship is not keeping up with it, apart from places like Dublin, maybe Cork, but certainly places like Waterford have no hope that we can attract a sponsor that will cover all of that. So sponsorship is a primary source of revenue.

'Your secondary source of revenue, I suppose, are gates. And gates are falling continuously. That needs to be grasped. Why is the attraction not there any more? I think a lot of it has to do with the level of facilities in the stadiums themselves. People in this day and age expect to have high-quality broadband, being easily able to access coffee and hot food at half-time, to take shelter from the rain and to be able to scroll on their phones when the ball is out of play. That's the reality.'

Elsewhere in this book Peter McKenna doubles down on that point. But Mac Murchú added another challenge:

'I wonder are our games at club level being marketed seriously enough? That's not a criticism, because we're all volunteers, but are they? There was a time when we'd all be hanging on for the local papers to see the draw for the local championship. An Rinn are playing The Nire at the weekend, but you saw that on the Wednesday in the paper and of course you were already preparing for Sunday at two o'clock.

'Now the games come and go – and that's happened to myself, by the way. I didn't even know the club were playing a game recently because I'm not involved at executive level any more. It's not even enough just to let people know that the games are on. I'm not a social media person; I'm like a lot of people, depending on the fifteen-year-old at home to tell me.'

The marketing around the games, even at a local level, then, could be better?

'You could have, say, Austin Gleeson versus Philip Mahony for Mount Sion versus Ballygunner in the Waterford championship. I've never seen that highlighted, a head-to-head clash, in the local marketing effort. You look at games happening at a national or international level to see what could be made of the games – I think that is something else that could drive attendances, because it's not enough any more to be depending on the pride of the parish.

'Some of us still have it, but people might decide to go for a nice meal than a match this evening, which was unheard of long ago. People might decide it's too cold to go, or a bit too wet to go, and that's a new reality. That is something else that worries me, falling attendances and the reasons for that.'

Mac Murchú raised another point, which may sit less comfortably with GAA people.

'It may be part of the same thing but once upon a time – and I'm not saying this was right or fair – players would cancel their weddings in order to play. If they could have been, then funerals would have been cancelled as well. Now it's a simple text: "Sorry, this holiday's been booked all year, I won't be at that game."

'I was an advocate always of fixtures being published so far in advance that players could organise their lives, but the point now is that for much, much smaller reasons, players are deciding not to turn up for an important championship game because there's something else on.

'Again, they have every right to do so, but the trend is in that direction. So then the logical conclusion to that is, will the GAA become a more recreational sport? And where does that then lead? If you start looking at the county level, where it cannot be recreational because it is more professional than it's ever been before, and there are teams of trainers and psychologists and whatever you're having yourself at enormous cost to try and gain that extra percentage point or two that will win a championship game for you. So then there's an even bigger difference between club and county in that the club is more recreational and the county is more professional.

'And then the other thing, of course, is where does this level of professionalism end? Do we keep going until we reach the Premier League-type professionalism? Do players make career choices based on being available to play for the county? The logical conclusion to that is, well, players will then have to be remunerated. But the amount of players in Ireland playing for thirty-two counties in two codes – where would the GAA get the money to pay for that? The money just isn't there. So where does that go? Does it go to, "Sure, I could play soccer with only half the hassle"?'

Introducing a different sport brings another dynamic altogether into play. When Dara Ó Cinnéide spoke to Tomás Ó Sé on the latter's podcast in 2024 the two Kerry icons lamented the loss of rising stars in the county to Australian rules football. At one level this probably raised an eyebrow in places like Down and Kildare, counties that lost promising youngsters to the AFL with little national reaction, not to mention the likes of Dublin and Cork, which for decades have seen players opt out of Gaelic games in favour of rugby and soccer. The idea that players going to Australia to play a professional sport is a problem for Ireland because it has become a problem for Kerry would find a chilly welcome beyond the boundaries of the Kingdom, particularly when one of its own exports, Tadhg Kennelly, was overseeing recruitment for the Australian game.

But as usual, Ó Cinnéide was able to articulate a wider truth about the talent drain better than most when discussing the departure of the talented Mark O'Connor:

'Most people . . . preface their remarks by saying, "Look, nobody could begrudge them that." And nobody does on a human level. But on an Association level, on a local GAA level, it's hugely disappointing – hugely disappointing when you invest time and effort and energy into players and you see them become successful and you want them to become successful and then they just get picked up.

'I think you [Ó Sé] got into a bit of hot water a number of years ago, even locally here in Kerry, people weren't too happy with stuff that you would have said about Mark O'Connor. Everybody, including yourself, would have wished him well in his endeavours and in his sport. But it's hugely disappointing for the Association, for the GAA. It is, as I'll reiterate, on a human level everyone's thrilled for these players.

'You know, most young athletes today, it's not like when we were twenty years of age. All we wanted to do was play for Kerry, really. I see it myself at local level, at club level here, and you know, that's to be expected. Life moves on and that kind of commitment to a kind of a tribe isn't there anymore. It's not. It's certainly not a huge motivating factor for a lot of the young athletes – and I call them athletes because that's how they view themselves – that play for Kerry or play for the club at the moment. They see it as . . . there's more to it. It's not that tribal thing. It's not. Their canvas is a bit wider. The world has gone a bit smaller, obviously, since we were their age, and they view it as progress, personal development, whatever you want to call it.

'But part of me dies inside every time I see it happening. And I don't say that lightly because I know the amount of time and effort that underage coaches have put into these lads. It's very hard to watch it happening and, you know, to be totally helpless in the face of that.'

To reinforce the point, when Ó Cinnéide's clubmate Marc Ó Sé appeared on TG4's *Laochra Gael* he told the *Examiner*, while on the publicity trail, that the drive to represent the county is missing:

I don't think it is there. It comes from the families, it does not just come from the player himself. I look back at the stories about Páidí [Ó Sé] when he was growing up. My grandmother would not have been into football, she was from Sligo. My grandfather Tommy Ó Sé would not have been that much into football, but our first cousin, Tom Long over the road, was, and maybe Páidí wanted to emulate him. It was probably someone within the family and my grandmother made sure she did everything in her power to ensure he achieved what he achieved. But I don't think it is in the county now. There is soccer, rugby, basketball, my young fella [Tadhg] now plays basketball, soccer as well as football and obviously he will have to make a decision in a couple of years as to what he will want to play . . .

It comes from within the family. You hear the stories about all these fellas who are going to go off to Australia and you would wonder is that level of passion there to achieve your boyhood dream, which is to play in the green and gold. I am not so sure. I think it has waned big-time.

EXISTENTIAL: CLIMATE CHANGE AND THE GAA

The challenges facing the GAA are the challenges facing modern Ireland, as we've seen. No surprise there, of course, but what about the biggest challenge facing the entire world, never mind Ireland? Climate change is clearly the test of our time. Bad faith actors such as Donald Trump notwithstanding, there is general acceptance that the entire planet is at risk from rising temperatures associated with the damage done by carbon emissions and the like.

As a result, extreme weather events are now far more common than ever before, with consequences for Gaelic games just as there are for every aspect of modern Irish life. For instance, Storm Éowyn hit Ireland with a vengeance in late January 2025, with disastrous results along the western seaboard in particular. The Connacht GAA Air Dome at the province's centre of excellence in Bekan, Mayo, felt the full impact of Éowyn. The red weather warning from Met Éireann was fully justified when strong winds and rain felled the innovative inflatable air dome. That wasn't the only playing premises affected by the storm. In Limerick, a section of the stand in the Kilmallock GAA grounds, Fitzgerald Park, was destroyed when winds ripped off a large section of its roof and came close to damaging parts of the town nearby: in pictures part of the canopy appeared to be hanging dangerously close to some property near the stand.

There were other impacts on the GAA world. Games such as the NFL Division 1 clash between Kerry and Donegal and the

Leitrim–Laois game in Division 3 were both postponed. In the former case road conditions prevented Jim McGuinness's side making the trip to Killarney, for a game that was due to throw in at 1.45 p.m. (There was some grumbling in Kerry about the fact that other teams from Donegal fulfilled their fixtures that weekend, though that might be better filed under 'habitual paranoia' rather than 'climate change impact'.) Leitrim versus Laois was affected by a different problem; electrical issues caused by Storm Éowyn meant a decision was made on the evening beforehand to postpone the game. A couple of NHL games also fell victim to the weather the same weekend. Westmeath's clash with Laois had to be postponed due to a frozen pitch, while Mayo's meeting with Cavan was also postponed because of storm damage to MacHale Park. That damage, primarily to the floodlights, meant the Mayo venue had to be assessed by health and safety officers to see if it was safe to host the Mayo footballers' game against Galway the following weekend.

That wasn't the only impact that Storm Éowyn had on the GAA community. Because swathes of the country were left without power after the storm, GAA clubs were quickly pressed into action as community hubs after Storm Éowyn moved on. Hence Kerry County Council designating a number of GAA clubs around the county as community centres that would provide assistance to householders across Kerry who were still without electricity. The intention was to allow those impacted by the loss of electricity, particularly vulnerable people who required humanitarian assistance, to access basic facilities such as charging points and showers, etcetera. The same happened in Cavan at Breffni Park, in Kildare at Clogherinkoe GAA and dozens of other club facilities all over the country. Credit where it's due, GAA clubs certainly weren't the only sports or voluntary organisations to open their doors.

Storm Éowyn produced historically strong wind gusts and was regarded as an exceptional event, fully justifying its status as a red warning event. It could conceivably be described as a once-off. But extreme weather isn't just a matter of wintry conditions. In July 2018 I was in Austin Stack Park, Tralee, to see Cork and Kerry contest the first under-twenty Munster final. The heat was searing. Literally. Water breaks were planned for the game and were embraced. It wasn't the first day that month when the boiling sun claimed a victim either; after the Munster hurling final that year between Cork and Clare Damien Cahalane of Cork had to be treated for symptoms of heatstroke.

Because it was that kind of summer, counties took action. The Offaly County Board introduced five-minute water breaks in each half for games played in hot weather, while a Tipperary referee decided unilaterally to halt a junior game in the county after 20 minutes to allow players to take on water. When Covid struck two years later the in-game water break became part of the matchday routine, but it was abolished when pandemic restrictions eased generally, specifically following the conclusion of the inter-county pre-season competitions in 2022. By then the water break had become a little bit discredited, growing synonymous with tactical readjustments and detailed instructions instead of hydration. Spectators weren't too happy with the breaks either, believing in some instances that their teams lost valuable momentum when the break was called or that opponents benefited disproportionately from a mini-coaching seminar held while the teams were supposedly taking on water.

But come the scorching summer of 2022 the water break was back, with some counties acting unilaterally to cool players as temperatures crept within sight of the 30-degree mark. The safety of players is paramount, obviously enough. If games are being played during the summer and the summers are getting warmer that needs to be addressed.

Rather than asking a county board official about the future, though, I asked a meteorologist. Not long after coming close to melting in Austin Stack Park I contacted Met Éireann's Gerald Fleming, who had then just fronted an RTÉ documentary on climate change which offered some catastrophic prospects, such as cities flooding. He acknowledged that climate change could have an impact on all sports not just Gaelic games:

'I think so, particularly those involving the winter months. In GAA terms I know there's some break in the winter months for football and hurling, but even that may have to be extended further. There have been a few occasions recently when the schedule's been upended by severe weather, with games being postponed. I would think it's probably a threat.'

In the TV documentary we saw what might happen if Cork and Dublin flooded. Not good news for sports facilities near rivers, obviously.

'That's true, though having playing fields beside rivers is often a good place for them. If they get flooded a couple of times a year it's not the end of the world – it's not like a house or a premises being flooded – so it's a good use of the space because that space can't be used for another purpose. Matches may have to be postponed occasionally because of flooding, but in real terms it's a trade-off that may be worth making as long as you can accept that having a playing field beside a river which floods occasionally has a built-in risk.'

Remove if you can the image of a new stadium under water and broaden your horizons. Fleming felt people were doing so already:

'It seems to be much higher in people's consciousness, it's something they seem to be factoring into their thinking, which is a good thing. And it's necessary, because there's no getting away from this, it's not a situation that's going to get any better. We have to accept what's happening and adapt our strategies accordingly.'

Have we accepted that? Changing climate patterns and more extremes of temperature, particularly heat, need to be considered by sporting bodies at all levels, and the introduction of mandatory water breaks needs to be a matter of priority, particularly if your sports are played during the summer.

Over thirty high school football players have died in America from heatstroke in the last twenty years, while heat-related illness kills more people in that country than hurricanes, lightning, earthquakes, tornadoes and floods. That may sound like an extreme comparison, but in an Ireland where the hottest month on record is a reliable summer headline it is not as far-fetched as it would have been twenty years ago.

Not when the entire notion of outdoor sports may itself be at risk. A couple of years back the 538.com website carried a fascinating report with a headline that told you everything about the content: 'Outdoor Tennis Could Be Sports' First Big Climate Change Casualty'. Writers Jonathon Braden and Matt Fitzpatrick used climate data models to map out possibilities for tennis in the coming decades, and the results were sobering.

At the 2050 French Open in Paris, players could experience a . . . temperature potentially reaching 90 [32.2°C]. The high when Nadal won his record-extending 14th Roland Garros title earlier this month [June 2022] was 72 degrees [22.2°C]. At Wimbledon, the groundskeeping crew will have to work extra hard to keep the lawns lush and tidy as it could feel like

102 degrees (38.8°C) in London in 2050. But that might feel like a reprieve compared with the 2050 US Open in New York, where the heat index could rise to 145 degrees (62.7°C).

The focus on players, understandable though it is, may result in slightly less emphasis being placed on another aspect of the climate crisis. Not the carbon footprint of GAA clubs per se – there are plenty of examples of clubs and stadiums taking the lead on environmentally friendly measures. O'Moore Park in Laois was earmarked for LED floodlights, which would cut emissions and costs alike, while Louth club Clan Na Gael, as part of the GAA's Green Club Programme, completed an energy-saving project aimed at achieving energy and maintenance savings of €10,000 per annum and a reduction in CO_2 emissions.

What about the carbon footprint of supporters? Every summer thousands of GAA fans take to the roads of Ireland to follow their clubs and counties. TV advertisements are fond of the image of supporters on trains or the Luas as they approach their chosen venues, but the roads don't lie. A huge proportion of those supporters drive to games all over Ireland, with a resulting spike in emissions.

It's worth pointing out that it's rare enough to see any mention of the vast carbon footprint of, say, an army of supporters following their team to an international soccer tournament held across several European countries or of fans who decide to go to Los Angeles for the Olympics. To be fair to Peter McKenna of Croke Park, he acknowledged the challenge in 2023 when chatting to RTÉ.

Fan travel would be the largest component of our CO_2 equivalent. We're in the region of 14,000 Co_2 equivalent emissions [roughly 64 per cent of their total emissions]. You compare that to food, which is 4,000. Cycling is an important component part, but you're not going to come from Kerry to a match on a bicycle. We're talking people from all over the country who are coming to Croke Park.

It was interesting that McKenna pointed to the options available: the GAA is not Iarnród Éireann, after all:

It's about a greener public transport. Dublin Bus are doing a fantastic job and Bus Connects is going to really help the city in making commuting by bus, Luas or DART more convenient and more efficient. We will start shifting the big CO_2 numbers by having a far more efficient public transport system and that's where the investment needs to go. I'd argue in favour of the metro and taking cars out of the city. Dublin is a small city.

There are other initiatives at play. Croke Park bought a farm in north Dublin to grow its own grass rather than having to import grass from the UK; 70 per cent of its food menus consist of produce sourced within fifty miles of Croke Park; the stadium has had an 'extensive' LED retrofit; and then there's water.

We're starting a water harvesting programme which will see water coming off the roof used to irrigate the pitch. We need to install a four thousand cubic metre tank, and that will then supply the pitch. Summers are going to get warmer and drought is more likely. Currently we're watering the pitch with potable [drinkable] water, which is unsustainable on a series of levels. This will eliminate that.

AI, A UNITED IRELAND AND MORE CHALLENGES

Looking a long way down the line can be dangerous in any line of business. Covid taught us that lesson. Still, opting out of long-term planning isn't an option for any organisation. What is lurking around the corner for the GAA – or around a couple of corners further down the line?

Integration is the obvious medium-term challenge, or opportunity, for the GAA, but part of the organisation's plan for the future should revolve around addressing some of the lingering issues of the present. The money sloshing around the Association isn't just a problem in and of itself. It's a problem because the mindset that surrounds it is so deep-seated now.

Ger Ryan saw it this way:

'I've always said that to an extent, if you put enough cones in the car, you could probably get around four or five counties and survive for fifteen or twenty years. How? By going to clubs and saying, "The last manager was useless, I'll sort that out," then you get a few years before you say, "Well, the players are useless" and you're on to the next place.

'What a club is failing to do is to set up a sustainable self-sufficient model. It's more, "Well, the club next door brought in Michael Moynihan, so we'll bring in Ger Ryan." But there's no focus on what's expected of the coach, the standards needed, all of that.

'Would a club be better off putting that money into

infrastructure, a gym maybe or inviting somebody to come in as a guest speaker and looking after their expenses?

'I was involved with Tipperary in logistics and player liaison for a few years. Somebody asked me to talk to a club manager in Tipp last year about how to approach management. I spent a couple of hours with him and he said to me – and I was shocked at this, though maybe I shouldn't have been – "What do I owe you?" Now, I have no issue with people getting expenses – officials and players – because there's a structure around that. But the minute we start straying outside that we get ourselves into trouble. People need to stand back and ask what's the value in this expenditure rather than saying (coming in under pressure as a club officer) that they have to spend this.'

Eradicating the 'What do I owe you?' attitude would be a significant help to the GAA. What else?

The controversies that surface in Irish life surface in the GAA too. In May 2024, when the GAA used artificial intelligence (AI) to create programme covers, artist Barry Masterson summed up the backlash on X when he said there were 'a ton of Irish artists who specialise in GAA illustration you could commission and support . . . things are tough at the best of times but I might have to pack it in at this rate honestly if this is what we have to look forward to'.

The programme covers concerned were appalling – weird thumbs, odd jerseys, helmet face-guards missing bars or disappearing into players' mouths and heads.

The GAA's response was bland enough ('We are constantly trialling new ideas for our match programme covers and this was a case of experimentation from our publishing partners' graphic designers'), but the backlash was pointed, showing that the GAA was taking work from Irish artists, specifically those specialising in GAA-related artwork, as Masterson pointed out, by definition a small group. At the time of writing the 'experimentation' hadn't been repeated.

One of the challenges coming for the GAA is probably one of the biggest questions facing Ireland as a whole. When news broke that the Revenue Commissioners were taking a close interest in the affairs of county boards around the country there were some, of course, that didn't come under their scrutiny. Those in Northern Ireland come under the purview of His Majesty's Revenue and Customs, which didn't appear to have the same focus on mileage rates and referee payments. Of course, at the GAA's 2025 Congress it was revealed that the 26 GAA county boards in the Republic of Ireland would be subjected to self-risk reviews following discussions between Croke Park and the Revenue Commissioners, and the other six counties were advised to undertake reviews as well.

The differences between the GAA in the Republic and the North of Ireland are sometimes unexpected, but often they're far clearer. Books have been written about the GAA and the Troubles, to take an obvious example, and even now that period casts a long shadow. At the same Congress mentioned above GAA President Jarlath Burns welcomed the family of Seán Brown, for instance. Brown was beaten and abducted by an LVF gang in 1997 as he locked the gates of Bellaghy Wolfe Tones Gaelic Athletic Club following a club meeting; he was then driven to a nearby lane and killed. Since then his family have attended court at least 57 times seeking justice, but early in 2025 the British government launched a legal challenge to overturn a court decision ordering a public inquiry into the murder, for which no one has ever been convicted. An earlier inquest heard that British state agents had been involved in the killing. At the 2025 Congress Jarlath Burns said:

Seán was one of our own and we make no apologies for doing all we can to assist the long-suffering, dignified but steadfast and resolute family that are the Browns. To do otherwise would be a failure to live up to our ideals and values as an organisation and as their extended family.

The place of the GAA in Northern Ireland can also be pointed out in the story of the GAA's biggest place in Northern Ireland. A timeline of the Casement Park saga is pretty grim reading.

- In 2006 plans were unveiled for a new 42,500-seater stadium for soccer, rugby and Gaelic games at the site of the former Maze prison. Three years later Democratic Unionist Party (DUP) sports minister Gregory Campbell scrapped that in favour of the sports bodies working up their own stadium proposals.
- In 2009 Ulster GAA proposed an upgrade of Casement Park and in 2011 Stormont agreed funding for major upgrades to Casement Park, Ravenhill and Windsor Park.
- In 2013 environment minister Mark Durkan granted planning approval for a 38,000-capacity Casement stadium but the next year the High Court quashed that approval after a legal challenge by residents.
- A 2015 report made recommendations on reviving the project and in 2017 Ulster GAA submitted a revised Casement planning application with a reduced capacity.
- In December 2018 a new business case on Casement was submitted by Ulster GAA to the Department for Communities with an estimated cost of around £110 million.
- In 2020 infrastructure minister Nichola Mallon recommended approval of the redevelopment of the stadium and in 2021 Casement Park was given formal approval.

- That year a residents' association launched another attempt to block the stadium's development but the attempt failed the following year.
- In 2023 works began, and Casement was linked to the British and Irish joint bid for the 2028 European football championships . . . until the British government withdrew from funding the redevelopment in 2024 because it feared the stadium would not be ready in time for the Euros. In a letter confirming that withdrawal British ministers pointed out the soaring costs of the project from £180 million (€213 million) when the Euro 2028 bid was awarded in October 2023 to potentially over £400 million (€473 million) in 2024 – though those figures have been contested.

One of those contesting the figures was GAA President Jarlath Burns. Early in 2025 he told reporters at the GAA's Annual Congress: 'I wish I could be optimistic, but unfortunately it's really only pessimism on Casement at the moment. The facts are that the person who we need to champion this [Casement Park] is Gordon Lyons. We are disappointed with how he has performed so far.' Lyons was the Northern Ireland Minister for Communities with responsibility for sport, and a member of the DUP.

Burns expressed his disappointment that Lyons had yet to attend a GAA match when he spoke:

Minister Gordon Lyons got an invitation whenever he became minister to a GAA match anywhere. He has yet to attend a match of hurling or football . . . I don't want to be negative, we have to work with these people, but I also want to be realistic about what we're dealing with and how challenging the landscape is for us, and for Stephen McGeehan

[Casement Park project lead], Brian McAvoy [Ulster GAA CEO], Tom Daly [Ulster GAA Stadium Board chairperson], people who are living this every day. They are becoming extremely frustrated.[*]

There is huge sympathy among GAA members in the Republic for what their counterparts in Northern Ireland have faced, and continue to face, when it comes to Casement Park. But now that a united Ireland is being discussed in calm, rational terms as a future possibility, how does the GAA fit into that landscape? Jack Anderson, who spent several years teaching in Queen's University Belfast, says:

'The funny thing about sport in Ireland is that apart from the FAI, almost every other sport on the island operates on an all-island basis. So of all aspects of Irish society that might be challenged by a united Ireland, the one that's probably best prepared for that prospect is sport.

'That's one way of looking at it. From my time in Belfast I often heard people ask what the difference between the GAA and the IRFU [Irish Rugby Football Union] was, and the joke answer was that the GAA never recognised partition and the IRFU never recognised that we left in the first place. But in the practical sense, for the GAA it would go from being part of the UK where it is very much a minority sport to being a mainstream sport immediately, and that would be huge. And – this with all due respect to Cork – Belfast would immediately become the second city in the country, with all sorts of implications for Casement Park, for instance.

'Partition has been in place for over one hundred years, and I think it's only when a southerner goes to the North that they see

---

[*] Lyons eventually attended a GAA game in May 2025.

how different it is. The health system is different, the education system is different, even the TV and radio are different. But one thing that is in common on the Catholic side is the GAA.'

Anderson was optimistic about the GAA in a united Ireland:

'I've travelled a lot around the North and the Republic, and the latter is a modern European economy, and nowhere is that better represented than in GAA clubs, ironically. That may not be quite the case in the North but if unification comes I think the GAA is uniquely placed to do very well out of it.

'There are other social and political issues, obviously, but that point is worth making. For many sports bodies there wouldn't be a huge difference given how they're set up and how they operate. In that sense it was really interesting to see the Olympics in Paris and how that played out, because the Irish team was a real mix of people from all over the island, the likes of Daniel Wiffen and Rhys McClenaghan.

'I played with Bredagh and you'd be going to play some match on the Ards peninsula – to get your arse handed to you, basically – and it was on those trips you'd learn something. Lads my age and older would be saying, "Oh, we'd always be stopped at this place," or "We would always be delayed going through this village," and then the next village would be a hurling village. I think we can forget that element of how it used to be.

'Then there's another twist in how southern GAA teams and players view the North. One time a team from Dublin came up for a challenge game and I remember sitting in our dressing room with the Bredagh lads, and one of them turned to me and said, "If one of them comes in and says, 'Keep it going up here, lads'" . . . And sure enough, the Dublin team manager came in and said just that. It was meant with sincerity but it's understandable that they'd get enough of that. The GAA means a lot in the North, maybe too much at times, but that's understandable.'

Absolutely it is. Stories such as Seán Brown's or Aidan McAnespie's or many others give a huge context here. But consider these comments from a prominent GAA official in 2023 on getting rid of the tricolour and 'Amhrán na bhFiann' at Gaelic games.

> Yeah, it wouldn't cost me a thought. Flags are divisive – do we need to say that any louder? If somebody was to propose in the morning that they were going to get rid of them all, it wouldn't bother me at all. It's not one of the core values that I have. It's an overtly political thing, it's something which is specific to national borders, it's nothing to do with culture. If I thought for a moment that suddenly [Ulster Unionist MLA] Tom Elliott would become our greatest fan I would get rid of them, surely.

The GAA official in question? Jarlath Burns.

It would take a braver person than this writer to puzzle out the ramifications of a united Ireland, which seems designed to test the notion of 'unintended consequences' to its limit. Could the GAA be a significant factor in helping that to become a reality? Gestures such as Burns's would surely help. He didn't make those comments when he was president of the Association, mind.

Which raises another question. What is the president of the GAA for?

When Rory Gallagher hit back at GAA President Jarlath Burns for getting involved in Gallagher's putative appointment with Naas GAA club, he made one significant point. Gallagher asked if Burns would take 'such direct personal action against others who find their private life the subject of social media commentary and hyperbole . . . The chilling effect of these actions cannot be greater. Mr Burns' actions not only undermine the very principles of fairness and equality to which the GAA is premised, but it sends a clear message that such dictatorial action can and will be taken, when the president sees fit.'

Given the storm he was embroiled in, it was unsurprising that Gallagher unleashed a broadside against the president of the GAA. Did he also raise a broader point, however? Should the president of the GAA insert himself into the controversy of the day? Burns himself might reasonably point out that the Gallagher situation, and the message it sent out regarding the values of the GAA, required an intervention – as he provided on *The Late Late Show*. The only problem with that logic is that every controversy and issue can be interpreted by someone as a small referendum on the values of the GAA and thus ripe for presidential intervention, yet obviously not all controversies draw that kind of attention.

Broader challenges faced by the GAA also demand attention and the president's focus. At around the same time that the Gallagher–Naas issue caught fire, for instance, Gaelic football was being remade courtesy of the FRC chaired by Jim Gavin. The FRC was widely seen as a brainchild of Jarlath Burns: was that a more appropriate use of the president's time? Or what is the president's time for? The obvious man to ask was Jack Anderson, whose knowledge of the GAA's rulebook would work well here. If the rules and regulations governing the games are generally cloaked in ambiguity, offering some leeway in interpretation, perhaps the role of president is similar.

'The president of the GAA can be a little bit like the president of Ireland sometimes. Some people go in and it's a reward for years of service, others go in and calm the waters like Paddy Hillery, some like the pageantry, and then you have others with the attitude, "Oh, this could be transformative" or who may have the attitude of a Michael D. Higgins.'

The comparison's an interesting one, not so much because of the general fondness for the man in Áras an Uachtaráin but because of his generous interpretation of his own constitutional obligations. Quite a few of Michael D.'s fans don't seem to consider the long-term implications of a president (of Ireland) overstepping the mark in this way. One of his replacements may not share the current president's outlook when following the precedent he's set on current affairs and may end up making pronouncements that enrage those now praising the current incumbent.

For many decades GAA presidents operated along the lines of Paddy Hillery, who was the epitome of a safe pair of hands on the tiller. Many opened club dressing rooms, presented cups and did their time on the rubber chicken circuit. But in recent years there seems to have been a drift towards presidents leaving a legacy of their own behind when they exit Croke Park.

'The legacy part may be attractive, but if you ask what the terms of reference are I think you'd struggle to find a document that outlines those for the president of the GAA.

'You look at the Ard Stiúrthóir of the GAA [Tom Ryan] and he's very good, but he's quiet. That's not a bad thing. The FAI's example shows the dangers of having a charismatic chief executive. But it is probably somewhat unusual that, for instance, the rule changes in Gaelic football were more or less driven by the president. You could certainly make the case that that's an executive function really, an operational decision. In that sense, while there probably are boundaries to what the GAA president can and can't do, those are pretty vague.

'None of that means someone like Jarlath Burns is doing a bad job either. He's different to other presidents; his predecessor, Larry McCarthy, would probably have seen his role as more ceremonial, for instance.'

Is this another instance of the GAA's functional vagueness operating to its advantage or a potential issue if a president takes office with a particular agenda? For Anderson the likeliest speed bump seems to be a blurring of the responsibilities.

'I think you have to be careful as president not to stray into the executive and operational fields. The term is very short – it's three years, but you could argue it's effectively two years.

'It's a strange one in that the role can be an unusual one, but the GAA has left it ambiguous, and maybe that was a creative enough decision. Jarlath is a good example in that he has defi-nite things he wants to do, and maybe at an executive level the GAA might be saying to itself, "Well, we could do with a bit of energy." To be fair to him it was only twelve months ago Jim Gavin and the FRC were getting started, and now we have the new rules in operation.

'Ultimately, is the president the chief executive or is he the chairman?'

Hence the power of that ambiguity. Is it too glib to say that the president can be both, or either, depending on which is more convenient? A more searching question might focus on the chance of a future president being incapable of either and what the GAA might have do in those circumstances.

* * *

What about other concerns, other challenges coming down the tracks?

Anthony O'Connor raised one issue that surfaces every now and again. What will head-high tackles in hurling lead to eventually?

'The size of the modern player is phenomenal – even club players are phenomenal in terms of their physique – but we just don't take stuff around the head and neck that seriously. I've seen hurlers strike players in the head area and been amazed they're not disciplined more stringently. If you look at a rugby match now, you know there's an acceptance that you just don't go anywhere near the head.

'What happens in our Association, and this is a major bugbear of mine, is someone in an All-Ireland semi-final can make a dangerous head-high challenge, and maybe he'll get sent off. But he'll get off the suspension. Even though a player came within three inches of paralysing an opponent for life he can't be removed from the big occasion?'

The legal aspect of this is addressed elsewhere in this book, as are the rhetorical justifications – 'Sure, he's not that kind of player, he shouldn't miss the biggest day of the year.' It all contributes to a casual attitude to something that should be taken very seriously indeed.

'I think it's dumb luck we haven't had a very serious neck injury. Guys have been killed playing cricket, after all, due to head injuries. I think the way the game is going, we have an opportunity now. We can learn from other sports. Players would adapt to stringent rules on high tackles.'

If it were brought in and the authorities stuck with it, warned that there would be no appeals entertained?

'Yes, there'd be pundits complaining and looking for "a game for men, nobody wants to see this", but after a while, the players would have internalised it and would just modify what they do. Everybody would come to accept it.

'But you can't really have accountability if you have a situation where players can get off suspensions. Remember, we market our games off these collisions. The week of the All-Ireland final you'll see the RTÉ montages, lads flaking into each other, the same in the Croke Park Museum.

'We're saying that the GAA player is as big as a professional rugby player, as fast if not faster than rugby players and will have the same levels of impact as rugby players. In that case it's magical thinking for us to say, "But we don't need to have the same precautions." It's magical thinking because on one hand, we're saying all these things, they're big, they're strong, but they're only amateurs, so . . . what?

'There's a decision to make on this. We can glorify the size and the speed of the players, the ferocious collisions, but we have a duty here to protect people when it does happen. And it's when rather than if, I think. When it does happen every-one will be sorry, there'll be regrets and benefit matches and all that sort of thing. Wouldn't it be a lot better if it just didn't happen?'

Ger Ryan of the Munster Council had a different concern.

'I think if you had a significant economic downturn that there would be consequences, obviously. We know the world works in economic cycles, things have changed and Ireland has absolutely become a wealthier country. But we had a downturn in the late 2000s and early 2010s, and that fundamentally changed the way people attended games. In 2024 we were delighted with forty thousand in Páirc Uí Chaoimh for Cork and Limerick and so on, but that was routine twenty-five years ago. At the height of Tipp and Clare, you'd be hoping to get a couple of tickets on a Saturday night.

'So all of those things change and have changed – we don't have the same numbers that we used to have. I think there is a whole economic reality there about what's affordable for people, and I think there's good affordability at present, but that may change.

'Another thing is reducing activity, and Covid is a good example there because we reduced the activity. And to my mind, not being scientific but if you looked at the team that trained in 2019 and then trained in 2021, you wouldn't see a whole lot of difference. Yet there was less activity. We know they trained less.'

The balance to find, then, as Ryan puts it, is between what appropriate training is and what affordable spending is:

'What are players who are doing the current training regime going to look like? There are scientific models that should allow us to be able to do that and present them with injury profiles in terms of the demands we're placing on our players. The public at a big game place a demand on those players to perform to a high standard; that's why they went to the game, so we have to balance that. But ultimately, you have to figure out what are we willing to pay and what's affordable. And for that we need to understand our long-term plans in relation to infrastructure, in relation to maintenance, in relation to how we want our clubs and our counties to operate. Then if you build an affordability model, I think you can start implementing caps and saying to any county, "You have to implement a cap, all counties have to do that."'

In Croke Park Peter McKenna saw a twofold challenge on the horizon:

'I think because the GAA is a movement it reflects Ireland, and the speed of change reflects the country. Could we have changed Rule 42 earlier, or Rule 27? I don't think so because the temperature was just right for those changes when they occurred and not before. If the GAA reflects Ireland it reflects the country like that also. Hindsight is great but I'd find it hard to see a change or decision that wasn't in tune with the time, the national mood of the time.

'If there's a challenge involved now it's in the work we need to do to include the new communities in Ireland. That requires a dedicated effort. I've seen stats recently that the indigenous population (which is a term I don't like but just for illustration) is decreasing and the number of newcomers is increasing. The Association is doing a good job on an individual club basis with new arrivals but I think we may need a more orchestrated approach.'

And a more strategic approach? A friend of mine likes comparing the GAA to the Catholic Church on the basis that both institutions share a fondness for long-term planning.

'We're absolutely like the Church and our history would point to a lot of commonality there between us. The essential difference is that the GAA can thrive in ambiguity. The Church couldn't. I think that's the difference. The Church battened down the hatches and became very adamant on certain issues – theological issues – while the GAA's ability to thrive on ambiguity helps us to keep going. The sense that if you're too strict, too regimented, there's a danger the brand breaks rather than bending.'

This was an interesting point, given the grappling about various issues within the GAA. Payments to managers was an obvious illustration – the ambiguities at play are almost overpowering – but McKenna's second challenge cut across that.

'I think we need to redefine what amateur status means, because there's too much value ambiguity there at the moment. What Jarlath [Burns] has set in play on amateur status is important because that's a core principle which needs to be redefined for life as is not life as was.

'Housing is an issue, obviously, and one point I'd make is that housing is created without accompanying facilities. We have no shortage of land, no shortage of resources, and the whole thing is still stuck. We could do this in the thirties and forties when we didn't have half the resources available to us, and when those housing schemes were built they had playing fields. I think some urgency here is badly needed, though I'm hardly the only one who's said or thought that.'

It's interesting that one contributor isolated a specific game-related concern, one picked on global economic trends and their potential impact on the GAA, and the last referred to Irish housing policy down the decades. That range of challenges, from internal to external, tells us as much about Ireland as the GAA; the fact that those challenges interact is another consideration, of course. According to Declan McBennett:

'I still think it continues to be the best community-based organisation in the country, and I think it will continue to have that role. But I also think it faces enormous challenges going forward in the same way society as a whole does, because while it's a microcosm, it's also a central microcosm of the broader society. I think it's going to come down to the same things in terms of population, urbanisation, rural depopulation, fixtures and finance. You can tweak the rules, you can tinker with them; you can look at the amateur status and you can talk about paying managers, but at the end of the day it's still about the level of participation.

'Participation and integration will be, to my mind, what defines the GAA over the course of the next twenty years, because that feeds into everything. How many pitches have you got? How do you buy the pitches? What facilities do you have? How do you get families to come along if they're standing frozen on the side of a pitch? Do you have a stand? Do you have a dugout? Do you have dressing rooms? Do you treat your girls differently from how you treat your boys, and do you treat the ladies differently to how you treat the men? What does that say about us as a society as a whole?'

McBennett leaned on his experience near home for illustration:

'We see it in Dublin on an ongoing basis, but I see it in rural Ireland. I see it in Armagh where the best facilities are all in the south of the county, largely; the clubs with two and three pitches are all within a ten- to fifteen-mile radius of each other. They're all driving on with each other and against each other, whereas the clubs largely in the north of the county are more urban. They're surrounded by housing estates and they don't have the capacity to expand, but their numbers are expanding through the roof.

'And we all know [from] the reports that have come out with regard to the GAA those demographics are going to be absolutely key whether it's the old Irish population or the new Irish population. It's just the population and it's going to grow exponentially. I look at the young Republic of Ireland teams and soccer is largely hoovering up a much greater proportion of the new Irish, as they're called, than the GAA. If you look at the team sheets of the Ireland under-seventeen or under-nineteen or under-twenty-one team, you can see a whole new Ireland. It's no longer Kelly and Quinn – the surnames are completely different. It's not that the GAA is failing in that, but definitely it is not picking up the same level, the same proportion of players. And again, that's largely driven by the new immigrant populations which are predominantly around the towns.

'In a very simplistic way the three issues identified around integration are a large part of what the GAA has to deal with, which is fixtures, finance and facilities.'

WHY? BECAUSE YOU LOVE IT

Tom Ryan explained the fundamental pull as well as anyone and in such a way that underlined its stubbornness. The likelihood that it will continue and will underpin the GAA.

'When you come down to it, you do it because you really love it. All the other stuff – tradition and heritage – is fine but it's secondary to the enjoyment. If you're not enjoying it what are you doing?

'I don't think people are going to the field thinking, "This is related to our ethos," it's because they enjoy it. Something that happened with Covid was that when the games were cut off I realised, for instance, that that cut me off from my network of friends. The loss wasn't "We won't win the championship" or even "There are no matches to watch," it was the loss of meeting people, that feeling of being part of something. And that has a value beyond football and hurling. I'm sure other organisations found the same, but when that wasn't available we missed it. A recurring theme – people saying, our village or town or part of the city will be fine, but it wouldn't be the same without this.

'And that's a good thing to say. I think we're different – I don't want to say better, and I don't know whether we are or not, but I get the sense that that is something the GAA can be proud of. I have respect for all the other organisations and what they're doing too.

'We mentioned an ecosystem, but an ecosystem has to be minded. Sometimes things can threaten us, both from within and from without, and you can't take for granted that it will always be like that.'

Tom Parsons looked at what the GAA and its players could offer the country in the future.

'We need to do things differently. I think the All Blacks changed a lot of thinking in sport with the idea that behaviours trump athletic identity. Back to my KPIs for a management team – if it's all about winning at all costs, that won't work; it has to be about more than winning an All-Ireland. It needs to be about elevating the behaviours, the values, the resilience we learn in sport. Why can't we select our thirty best players and say it's about more than athletic excellence, it's about representing your county and inspiring people in your county?

'When we did workshops as Mayo footballers, when we were giving it all, it was never about maximising your athletic identity so much as inspiring the people of Mayo. That helped us find the drive, the "why" behind it.

'Some people might not agree, but role modelling has a place, I think. Sport can be a better vehicle for good in the world. I like how sport has evolved to reflect values, and the GAA in the future should look at KPIs where role modelling is a key feature.

'But again, that needs investment and time for developing off-field stuff about values and behaviours. I appreciate the expectation on amateur players is unbelievable, and the public scrutiny may not be fair, but if someone goes on a journey as an inter-county player and you come out a better person with a better character, then it will serve that individual better as well.'

And more immediately? Peter McKenna was talking months before the Pittsburgh Steelers rolled into town: a harbinger of a bright future, he thought.

'If we do this well as a city we could be looking at six to seven games over a decade. This would be a massive tourism pull; it would cement ties to what's a very important market with the number of American companies here through FDI [foreign direct investment] and the Irish companies employing people in the US. The NFL is the most powerful sport on the planet in terms of power, eyeballs, connections. It's a great coup to have them. The week after next [February 2025] they're sending seventy people here to see how we do our business. Seventy. We have four people in our events department.'

(Those plans take time, of course. McKenna explained how much time was involved: 'Organising this was a lot of hard work. In my office I have a proposal we sent to the NFL in 2012, which had the approval of then Minister for Sport Leo Varadkar. These things take a long time.')

At another level of the GAA the sense of community remains an opportunity and a challenge. 'Even the word community is hugely important, I think,' said Dara Ó Cinnéide.

'So much so that the Gaelic Community Association might be worth considering as a name or part of the name, it's so important. Around here in the Gaeltacht, as is the case with other parts of the country, you could ask an honest question: "Is the social cohesion that strong?" There might be a sense of romanticism abroad about Gaeltacht communities, that we back each other all the time, but we ourselves live gated existences like everybody else. We're as individualised and private as people elsewhere in Ireland, where you ring your neighbour to say you might call over rather than just calling in.

'That old idea of bóthantaíocht, coming in through the half-door when you see the smoke coming out of the chimney, that is long gone and is as true of the Gaeltacht as it is of Dublin 4. And that's where the GAA is great because when you move to a new area where you don't know anyone, it's the obvious first step. My own daughters dropped out of Gaelic football lately and I was saying to them, "Would ye not keep it up because when ye go to college it'll open up so many doors and help ye make friends?"

'Loneliness, exclusion, social isolation – those are real issues we now deal with, and the GAA club is an obvious way to deal with that. When Covid hit the country the GAA was mobilised within a couple of days: "You can't do your shopping? We'll do that for you." All of that. And that should be a reflex action all the time with the GAA, but I'm not sure if it is any more. That's a big concern of mine.'

Well, it's the GAA: even when you're positive you have to be concerned. But Ó Cinnéide raises a very important point. The GAA's position in the community is a strong one, but should it be formalised?

ALWAYS

In writing this book I wanted to show where the GAA is, where it might improve and what it can expect in the future. Much of the time that was done without explaining what it means. That's because defining the GAA, and the particular grip it exerts on people, is a fool's errand. Everyone's GAA is different, and everyone's is valid.

Dara Ó Cinnéide recalled a conversation he'd once had with another Kingdom great, Mickey Ned O'Sullivan, who'd played in the great Kerry–Dublin rivalry of the seventies.

'I remember saying to Mickey Ned that I'd watched the Anton O'Toole documentary, and one scene struck me in particular. The former Dublin players were sitting out near the sea somewhere, chatting on a sunny day, and David Hickey made a great point. He said, "We always showed up for each other." Funerals, parties, outings – and they're touching eighty years of age now – they always turned up for each other. Ever since, I've used that line in the Gaeltacht dressing room. I've begged them: show up for each other. Don't just drop your gear bag and play. Show up for each other. And that's the GAA. You go to funerals, you make yourself available, you end up doing things that are beyond what's reasonable or rational because you want to show up for your teammate.'

That commitment to each other is a natural element of the GAA. As a community it's a broad one. When the Tipperary hurler Dillon Quirke died suddenly on the playing field in 2023 there was an outpouring of grief, unsurprisingly: Quirke was just 24 years old. The last man he marked at inter-county level was Shane Kingston of Cork, and the two swapped jerseys at the final whistle. When Kingston heard the news he drove to Tipperary to return the blue and gold jersey to Dillon Quirke's family. He wasn't asked and he didn't have to be persuaded; it was obvious to him that that was the right thing to do.

The GAA's values may be threatened on occasion – at times, in fact, they seem to be tested to the very limit – but there is also a stubbornness that gives those values permanence. It can be seen at a thousand funerals which local clubs help to organise and the quiet word from a chairman or secretary to the bereaved family afterwards.

It's visible in the generosity when a local cause is flagged: when Clare youngster Joel Slattery suffered life-changing injuries at a club training session in 2024, the resulting GoFundMe campaign raised more money that year than any other appeal on the platform.

At the start of the pandemic I rang a high-ranking GAA officer to discuss the Association's reaction: he only agreed to detail the work his club was doing in the locality – visiting the elderly, organising grocery shopping and deliveries – if I promised not to use his name in the story.

All the tensions and challenges mentioned in this book will be familiar to GAA members everywhere. Because of that it was relatively easy to find one place where most of them intersected. Some years ago St James' GAA club in Ardfield, west Cork, collected its first junior title, beating Ballinascarthy in a closely fought final at Timoleague. I spoke to the chairman, Niall O'Sullivan, a couple of weeks after that game, and the conversation pulled together a lot of the matters articulated in this book long before I thought about writing it.

For instance, O'Sullivan said geography hindered the club; they were squeezed between two bigger outfits, Clonakilty on one side and Carbery Rangers of Rosscarbery on the other. The main reason they had an under-sixteen hurling team in 2019 was that a few lads from Rosscarbery wanted to hurl, so the numbers worked out. 'But in football terms we didn't have the numbers to field at under-twenty-one, minor, under-sixteen,' said O'Sullivan. 'Our next strong team coming through would be around under-fourteen, under-twelve; we're fairly okay there, but in general terms things are barren.'

The club's base in Ardfield is in a stunningly beautiful part of the country, but it's also remote. Many people have to travel to Cork to work, and it's difficult for people to get planning permission in the area. The consequent lack of families affects the community as a whole because it affects enrolment in the school and that affects the GAA club and all the other organisations in the community. O'Sullivan said the community was 'trying to hold on to the teachers in the schools, which is disappointing'.

For all that, he and his club were optimistic, and he pointed to their advantages. They were in a great location with terrific facilities, having spent €1.3 million to upgrade and improve their pitch and premises. When I asked if they ever lost heart getting teams out and sourcing players, he was defiant.

'That part isn't hard, in fairness. The kids want to play, they want to join in and have fun with us. We have a nice bond between the underage kids and the adults; it's great that they all know each other. How many sporting organisations could say that their under-sixes, their under-eights would know the adults playing for the club? Not many clubs could state that, but it's what the GAA does. It connects all those people.'

He also pointed out that the other organisations in the area supported St James', particularly when they won their title: practical co-operation, you might call it.

'In fairness, the other sports clubs in the parish were among the first people who were on to us when we won. The minute the match was over they were texting us with congratulations and a lot of them were at the final itself. I saw them in the crowd and at the celebrations. We try to support them as well because at the end of the day we're all pulling from the same resource; we all need to help each other out. There has to be co-operation between the groups when it comes to teams because the numbers are so small.'

That co-operation enables all clubs and sports to survive, which in turn benefits the communities where they operate.

Integration, another live topic in this book, was a practical matter for St James'.

'We have girls playing, and we rely on them. We need them to make up the teams. It's great because they push on the lads and the lads push them in turn. The bond between them because of playing together up to under-ten, under-twelve is great; it's completely natural because they're just so used to playing sports with each other. Allowances aren't made, mind you – a girl will get a belt of a shoulder or a flake across the legs if the sliotar is by her feet as quick as a boy.'

O'Sullivan was keen to spread the credit to the people who make the club work and to the administrators willing to make local arrangements to help kids to play.

'It's been great, but that's all down to the people who are willing to come out in all weathers to teach them the skills, to go and get kids back involved if it looks like they're dropping out . . . It doesn't just happen. It's work that has to be done.

'Fair dues to the GAA, too; it has recognised the particular problems clubs like ours have. Most of our teams are thirteen-a-side, because we just wouldn't have the numbers for fifteen-a-side. At under-fourteen we have sixteen players, so if two or three of them are gone away for any reason we'd be in trouble. Rebel Óg said recently that they'd look at catering for nine-a-side as well for clubs that are struggling. That's fantastic, because it keeps people in the sport and gives them the opportunity to play the games.'

When the junior team got back to the clubhouse with the cup, they had company. The club had also won under-fourteen and under-twelve trophies, so the victorious teams celebrated together. As a club.

'We brought all the kids with their cups up there and welcomed them in with the juniors. We didn't single out any team, because every cup we win is as important as the other.

'In the pictures, even, we made sure the junior lads were in the background and the under-tens, under-twelves, under-fourteens were in the front. They're our future. In a place like ours the GAA club is the centre of the community and if we lost it something very important would be lost.'

O'Sullivan spoke for a thousand clubs when I asked him about the future.

'No matter what happens in St James' GAA club, that spirit will never be beaten. We will always find a way to get the teams out, to get the youngsters out to play for us. The spirit is there always. Always.'

Always.

ACKNOWLEDGEMENTS

Thanks to everyone for their help with this project and in particular the people who were generous with their time and energy in discussing these matters (by which I mean listening to me flail around), whether on or off the record.

In particular my thanks to all in Gill Books for their support and patience: Sarah Liddy, Isabelle Hanrahan, Patrick O'Donoghue and all the team.

Thanks to others for their encouragement with this project and many others: Diarmuid O'Donovan, Colm O'Callaghan, Eddie O'Donnell, Dave Hannigan, Gary Murphy and many more.

Thanks also to my brothers and sister for their support over the years. I presume they won't mind special thanks to my nephew Daniel Murray for a great weekend in Barcelona.

Time was when two of the most important people I thank here were too small to be aware of the GAA. While I was writing it one of them got fond of shouting, 'Don't take that off him, Robert Downey' at matches, while the other advocated relentlessly for Shane Kingston to make Cork's first fifteen. Clara and Bridget, don't ever forget: it's amazing to be young. Thanks also to their grandparents Bobby and Breda.

If I were to thank Marjorie for everything I'd end up filling another book. It's appreciated. All of it.

And Donie and Mary. Always.

Hang the jersey on the gate.